From Silent Witnesses to Active Agents

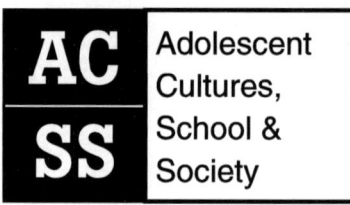

Joseph L. DeVitis & Linda Irwin-DeVitis
GENERAL EDITORS

VOL. 55

The Adolescent Cultures, School and Society series
is part of the Peter Lang Education list.
Every volume is peer reviewed and meets
the highest quality standards for content and production.

PETER LANG
New York • Washington, D.C./Baltimore • Bern
Frankfurt • Berlin • Brussels • Vienna • Oxford

John Smyth & Peter McInerney

From Silent Witnesses to Active Agents

Student Voice in Re-engaging with Learning

PETER LANG
New York • Washington, D.C./Baltimore • Bern
Frankfurt • Berlin • Brussels • Vienna • Oxford

Library of Congress Cataloging-in-Publication Data

Smyth, John.
From silent witnesses to active agents: student
voice in re-engaging with learning / John Smyth, Peter McInerney.
p. cm. — (Adolescent cultures, school and society; vol. 55)
Includes bibliographical references and index.
1. Children with social disabilities—Education (Secondary)
2. High school students—Attitudes. 3. Alienation (Social psychology)
4. School failure—Prevention. 5. Motivation in education.
I. McInerney, Peter. II. Title.
LC4069.4.S69   371.9'0473—dc23   2012003605
ISBN 978-1-4331-1374-1 (hardcover)
ISBN 978-1-4331-1373-4 (paperback)
ISBN 978-1-4539-0767-2 (e-book)
ISSN 1091-1464

Bibliographic information published by **Die Deutsche Nationalbibliothek**.
Die Deutsche Nationalbibliothek lists this publication in the "Deutsche
Nationalbibliografie"; detailed bibliographic data is available
on the Internet at http://dnb.d-nb.de/.

The paper in this book meets the guidelines for permanence and durability
of the Committee on Production Guidelines for Book Longevity
of the Council of Library Resources.

© 2012 Peter Lang Publishing, Inc., New York
29 Broadway, 18th floor, New York, NY 10006
www.peterlang.com

All rights reserved.
Reprint or reproduction, even partially, in all forms such as microfilm,
xerography, microfiche, microcard, and offset strictly prohibited.

Printed in the United States of America

Table of Contents

	Acknowledgments	vii
1	Framing Up the Book	1
2	'Speaking the Unpleasant': Argument and Context	7
	Framing up some unpleasant realities—about schooling and young people	8
	How all of this impacts young people	11
	What then, are we to make of all this in re-thinking schooling around young people?	14
	Geographies of exclusion…in the lives of young people	16
	Unsettling dominant 'deficit' and 'at risk' view of disengagement from learning and schooling	20
	Some troubling questions and the need for courage	23
3	Hearing the Voices of Young People: Our Method and Approach	27
	'This is going to get pretty messy'	27
	Something about the participants, their contexts, lives and circumstances	29
	Listening with intent—ethnographic interviewing	31
	Positioning ourselves—advocacy research	33
	Making sense of it all: Bringing empirical research into conversation with critical social theory	36
	Real young lives—the incredible power of portraiture	37
	'People can be very nasty'	39
	Closing remarks	40
4	Becoming Re-connected: Storylines from the Fieldwork	41

	Introduction	41
	Re-engagement with learning beyond the mainstream	43
	Becoming re-connected to education	47
	Becoming somebody: Connecting to self	49
	Projecting a sense of hope and possibility	52
	Being in control	54
	Humanizing relationships: Connecting to others	56
	Serving your time and starting afresh	59
	Taking harassment seriously: 'They handle things differently here'	60
	Developing support networks: Connecting to communities, resources and opportunities	62
	The stigma of young parenthood	63
	Social networks	64
	Engaging pedagogies: Connecting to learning	66
	'The way we learn is different to school'	67
	Learning different kinds of things in different ways	69
	Having fun: learning that is personable and enjoyable	70
	'We get to have a say'	72
	Have these re-engagement programs made a difference?	73
	Concluding remarks	77
5	Hearing the Story Again—This Time from Adults	79
	Introduction	79
	Teachers' stories	80
	Visions of success	81
	Unauthorized methods	83
	Connecting to young lives	87
	Making a commitment to the humanity of students (Ayers, 2004)	89
	'Significant others' stories	91
	Youth housing and education	92
	Juvenile justice and schooling	94
	Youth counseling	96
	Concluding remarks	97
6	Dreams of a Different World: Changes to Policy and Practice	101
	Appendix: Summary of Student Interviews and Re-engagement Programs	115
	References	117
	Subject Index	125
	Author Index	135

Acknowledgments

Writing a book can at times feel like a lonely and very individualistic process, but in the end it is only possible because of the largely unseen contributions and support from a wide range of people and organizations—some of which we cannot name here for reasons of confidentiality.

We do wish to express our considerable appreciation to the Australian Research Council (ARC) for the Linkage Grant that supported the fieldwork reported upon here. No matter what we might think of governments of whatever political persuasion we are indeed fortunate in Australia to have an independent publicly funded agency like the ARC that continues to steadfastly support our research.

To the Victorian Department of Education and Early Childhood Development (DEECD), Grampians Region, our industry partner in this research, we express our appreciation for funding support and the unfettered access to garner our accounts from young people.

To the various Neighborhood and Community Houses, local and regional agencies and Departments, we thank them for their assistance.

To the School of Education and Arts, University of Ballarat—one of the smallest universities in the country—we are grateful for the precious 'oasis' in which to pursue our joint writing, something not to be taken for granted.

To Chris Myers, Joe DeVitis and Linda Irwin-DeVitis (Series Editors), Bernadette Shade, and the incredible team at Peter Lang Publishing, we thank you for continuing to think we have something important and worthwhile to say.

To the courageous young people who so articulately shared some remarkable stories about their lives and what it meant to find places in which to re-invent themselves educationally speaking, we are considerably indebted, and we hope that we have truly rendered your stories accurately.

To our long-suffering wives, we thank them most profoundly for putting up with two old guys who should be well and truly retired!

Finally, to Solveiga, who for some inexplicable reason continues to 'hang in' with all of this, and provides cheerful disposition, remarkable administrative and organizational support, and does unbelievable *in situ* transcripts, not to mention magic with organizing the textual and reference materials—you are not available to marry anyone else!

CHAPTER 1

Framing Up the Book

The title of our book is an opportunistic take, in part, from the highly acclaimed and popular BBC television crime and forensic pathology series *Silent Witness*. Sometimes gruesome, the series is always about gripping accounts of how a forensic pathology team dismembers dead people on dissecting tables in solving major crimes. What is interesting for us, in this, is that like its TV namesake, young people in schools are treated with pathological and forensic detachment in diagnosing what is allegedly wrong with them and how they got to be that way. In the process, they are officially denied what amounts to a voice in a context in which their lives, families, neighborhoods and communities are being scrutinized and examined in policy terms for all manner of deficiencies, and then reconstructed in ways that will supposedly make them wholesome again, while also improving national economic competitiveness. This is the stuff of pure fantasy! If only it were that simple. The reality is that young lives, especially those from the most marginalized of contexts, are far more complex than can be accommodated by policy that is winged from a distance. Young people are not inert materials to be prodded, poked and pontificated upon—they are active, live agents that have viewpoints, aspirations and designs for their futures, which they are not at all reticent in speaking vociferously into existence.

The existential contemporary reality is that young people in Western countries, especially those from the most disadvantaged side of the social gradient, are giving up on and disconnecting from schooling at an alarming and distressing rate, and with dire individual and social consequences. In this respect it might be more accurate to say that the mainstream institution of schooling has given up completely on those young people who present as the most difficult and exacerbated cases—those from urban and disadvantaged contexts and those with the most complex lives.

What we have then, is a growing mismatch between what politicians and policy makers argue schools ought to be doing, largely for the economy, and on the other hand, the reality of what young people themselves want from schooling in terms of their identity formation, and what they are prepared to endure and commit to within the institution of formal schooling. In many respects, there is a very uneasy standoff between these two positions, with no early signs of the misalignment being about to end any time soon.

We think this book comes about at a most propitious time. At precisely the time educational policies are becoming increasingly muscular in the way they bear down in terms of national testing regimes, managerialism, mandatory accountability standards, and all manner of consumerist and performativity measures—young people are 'speaking back' in increasing numbers on issues to do with the relevance of schooling to their lives, and in some quarters at least, there are the beginnings of a glimmer of hope that things may be officially changing for the better for some of these young people. The complete irony is that the same institution and system of schooling that has marginalized, alienated, damaged and excluded these young lives from fulfillment through schooling, and which resulted in their becoming lost to schooling in the first place, may have begun to envisage a set of quite different ways of re-connecting these young people to learning.

Sometimes ideas are simply obdurate. The general perception is that when young people fail in school, it is their fault. Schools may not be working because young people are not listened to and do not have a say over their learning. The effects of this miscuing are palpable and on display everywhere—unacceptably large numbers of young people find schooling to be irrelevant and intolerable. Meanwhile, there is a huge policy blindness and deafness to what is going on among the people charged with the responsibility for what transpires in schooling. If we are only partially accurate in our assessment of this, and what we are arguing is in fact the case, then this is a book that may have considerable longevity indeed!

What we describe in this book from the vantage point of a cadre of young people on whom schooling has officially given up, is what was happening to them in their lives at the time, what occurred as a result, and how they found their way back into learning under a very different set of conditions to those that repelled them in the first place, and what this re-connection meant to their lives, their health and their life chances. For no other reason, we believe these accounts make fascinating reading, because of the prominence we have been able to give the voices of young people themselves!

Suffice to say that we believe that this is a book that has within it a "big idea"—and it is very poignantly conveyed in and through the title. Young people are the most salient witnesses of what occurs in schools and classrooms, yet at the same time, they are the most marginalized and excluded. This is a truly shocking situation. Imagine where our courts and legal system would be if the most important witnesses were ignored, silenced, or muzzled? Clearly, the legal system would collapse, yet our school systems blunder on blissfully unaware of or willfully ignoring the voices of those who know the most—young people.

The central defining idea in this book is that young people have something valuable and worthwhile to say about schooling, its shortcomings, its merits, its relevance to their lives, and what they know about it as active and informed participants. What this book does is take us up close to the lives and stories that young people have to tell about what is involved in disconnecting from school, and what the existential experience has meant to their lives and life chances. The interesting twist here is that the 100 or so young informants in the study, were ones who had not only been repelled by school (or in many cases propelled out of school), but they had all found their way back into learning—under conditions very different from those that led them to leave in the first place. We are, therefore, able to provide stories of young people who have moved back and forth across the learning boundary, and the contrasts are very stark indeed.

As is usual in books like this one, there is quite an extensive story to be told about the magnitude and extent of the problem, but we don't dwell excessively on that—nevertheless it is important to provide a sharp synoptic state-of-the-art view at the outset of the alarming and damaging effects of schooling on the lives of many young people, and we do that in chapter 2, by facing up to some very unpleasant realities. In framing up the rest of the book in this opening chapter, we also say something about how we came to be investigating this topic, and of the positive and affirming accounts that unfold as young people told us about a very different space from the ones they were in when mainstream schooling failed them. What we have to tell here is akin to going from the pits of despair—and many of the young people we encountered in the study were in some very bad spaces—to getting prepared to hear some incredibly uplifting and positive accounts as some insightful young people mapped out very different futures for themselves as they reconstructed their lives, often with some quite remarkable and inspiring 'teachers' and other adults.

The kind of unpalatable truths we point to that are not always matters of polite conversation, like: how as a society we have become deeply implicated in constructing a system of schooling that is deliberately designed to assign large numbers of young people to the militarized category of 'collateral damage'. The kind of troubling questions that we suggest need to be further addressed are:

- What kind of society are we creating?
- Who are schools working for?
- What are the consequences of inequality?
- What kind of future are we creating?
- Is this sustainable?
- Are we at risk of losing a generation?

Where these questions lead us to is a consideration theoretically, philosophically and practically of issues to do with: exclusion, marginalization, alienation, disaffection and hopelessness—and what needs to be done about them.

Chapter 3 is about our method and approach and, invoking the words of one of our young informants, it might be seen in some quarters as being 'pretty messy'—which is probably too harsh a judgment of ourselves! What we reveal here are some of the aspects of the nature of our research craft—how we designed our study, how we undertook it, the tensions and contradictions, and how we struggled to make sense of and honorably represent the material we collected from young people. We believe that one of the reasons young people's lives and accounts are pushed into the background, ignored, erased, or given less attention than they deserve, is that researchers are either unprepared or ill-equipped to engage in the risk-taking necessary to yield up vibrant accounts of young lives. It requires considerable courage and skill to do this, and in synoptic form, what we deal with in this chapter are matters like:

- Our informants—their lives and contexts
- Listening with intent—through ethnographic interviewing
- Positioning ourselves—in what we call 'advocacy research'
- Making sense of it all—by sifting and sorting into themes
- Revealing real young lives—the incredible power of portraiture as a research approach
- Reflecting it back—tuning back into the conversations with young lives.

Chapter 4 is in a sense the heart and soul of the book, in which we refer to the accounts of the young people as 'storylines'. This is where we reveal though portraiture, largely on the terms of young people themselves, something of what was happening as a result of them disconnecting from school, of the sense of loss but also relief, but more importantly, how they came to re-discover a passion for learning under a very different set of circumstances to that which had expunged it. We describe something of the archeology of the programs, the people, and the experiences that turned these young lives around. We are also sanguine in revealing the tensions and unresolved issues. There are some very raw and sad accounts here, but equally some incredibly optimistic stories of success in working against the odds.

In chapter 5, if we were positivist researchers, which we avowedly are not, this is where we could be seen to provide some triangulation or validation of the accounts provided by the young informants in chapter 4—we have called this, appropriately, 'hearing the story again—this time from adults'. Here we rehearse some incredible stories of educational re-engagement and social connectedness from 'significant others' in the lives of the young people we interviewed—teachers, program leaders, community/youth/social workers, community policing, and others—all of whom have seen the low points and the high points in the quite remarkable journeys of these young people. We drew back from having discussions with parents and families, logical as it might seem to have done so. Our reasoning was that we did not want to run the danger of severely breaching or compromising, in some instances, the high level of trust accorded to us by these young people in so candidly revealing their stories. Our account may be considered to be somewhat incomplete because of this omission, but it is one we are prepared to live with given the importance we placed on maintaining trust.

Finally, we conclude in chapter 6 with a more upbeat finale as to what might be possible in what we call 'daring to dream of a different world—changes to policy and practice'. As befits our style of research, we are not in the business of providing lists of 'recommendations', choosing instead to highlight what we regard as some of the large unresolved tensions—and we do this by working through some of the dimensions of inequality that have to be confronted and struggled with, if the process of schooling is to be a more *socially just alternative* to that which is currently in place for so many young people.

CHAPTER 2

'Speaking the Unpleasant'

Argument and Context

The somewhat provocative title for this chapter is borrowed from Chavez & O'Donnell (1998) whose book of essays on multiculturalism is dedicated to the memory of Paulo Freire, and their sub-title of the 'politics of (non)engagement' is a most apt lead-in to the substance or our own work around how young people are being increasingly displaced from schooling. To establish our position unequivocally from the start—we regard the displacement of young people from schooling as not being the result of mere accident or something that occurs naturally, but rather as a consequence of the operation of powerful forces that are far from innocent. These are not matters in respect of which we can collectively remain detached, nor should we.

To draw attention to the alarming proportion of young people in affluent countries who are being left out, excluded, marginalized, alienated, and damaged by schooling despite all of the political posturing and muscular rhetoric to the contrary about *No Child Left Behind* (in the US), *Every Child Matters* (in the UK), and their equivalents in other countries, is not something by and large that is countenanced in polite conversations. If it is done at all, it is done in private and in hushed tones. To face up to the reality that a significant portion of our young people are being relegated to a bleak and dismal future, would be a monumental admission of failure on our part as adults that something is seriously awry in our wealthy and so-called advanced societies—but that's the state we are in, and there are a host of reasons for our reticence:

- the root causes afflicting young people's futures are portrayed as residing in the distant machinations of global restructuring and are therefore beyond our immediate reach or control in ways that we cannot do anything about;
- the problems of disaffected young people can be hidden, and when they do surface at inopportune moments and in inconvenient ways, then we individualize the problem by blaming young people, and there are lots of examples of this kind 'demonizing' and 'moral panic';
- in a sense we are able to 'export' the problem of getting to directly know what is going on in the turmoil of young lives, by further distancing ourselves as adults from any dysfunctional aspects by resorting to hands-off, technical, programmatic 'solutions'. In other words, we are able to avoid having the deep relational conversations that might cast light on the complexities of what is occurring from the point of view of young people themselves, by arguing that problems are being handled systemically;
- there is the widespread view that young people need to 'work it out for themselves', after all their parents did, and they have to make their way meritocratically in the world—never mind that the tectonic plates of capitalism have been seriously tilted against them in ways that their parents never had to encounter or deal with. To put it most directly, young people are seen as needing to experience the harsh realities of an increasingly fractured and fragmented world and sort out where they fit in it.

Framing up some unpleasant realities —about schooling and young people

One of the problems in being swept up in a vortex is that it is not always possible to see clearly what is happening, and there is a sense of awe and fascination about the power of nature. There is a lot of energy, much noise and rotation, turbulence and swirling action, and a profound sense of being carried along by forces in ways that you don't understand. The metaphor of the vortex very much captures the situation we are currently in with regard to schooling. There is much activity and reform being imposed on schools, most of it being orchestrated from a long distance away, by forces and for reasons we don't fully understand.

'Speaking the Unpleasant'

As citizens we have been excluded from being part of the conversation about what our schools are supposed to exist for, how they are supposed to operate, and for whom. Largely without our permission we have been interpellated into schools as 'consumers' who exercise 'choice' as to where we send our children to school, and in order to ensure we secure the 'best deal', we have been invited to force schools to be 'competitive' with one another in order to raise standards, ensure value for money, and enhance the national skills base in securing an internationally competitive economy. It all sounds very logical—until we begin to step outside of its own logic and ask some difficult questions.

To put it bluntly, our schools have been hijacked, and to a large degree we have knowingly been complicit in allowing this to occur and have offered little or no resistance. The consequence of our indifference and inaction is very much on display, as one of us put it presciently over a decade and a half ago (see Smyth & Shacklock, 1998, p. 1), and it is worth citing here in some detail because the illustration and the commentary on it is helpful:

> The HOPI Indians inhabit the mesa or plateaued mountains of Arizona. They have a centuries-old ritual of rising before dawn and "praying the sun up".
>
> Some American anthropologists came along and suggested that just for one morning they might sleep in and miss their prayers and see what happened.
>
> Incredulously the Hopi replied: "What, and plunge the whole world into darkness for the sake of your stupid experiment?"
>
> Over the past decade we have undergone a cultural experiment at the suggestion of economic scientists. Simply stated, they proposed that an increasingly competitive global economy required the floating of our dollar, the deregulation of our financial system and the reduction and removal of tariffs.
>
> Public employment and public spending had to be cut drastically and much sharper inequalities of income or salaries embraced.
>
> Higher levels of national unemployment were necessary for low inflation and a growing economy, and, in private enterprise, contractual, insecure employment had to be accepted.
>
> In short, competition had to replace protection and cooperation as the prime public ethic.
>
> Those who queried this path were denounced as irrational, naive and as foolish as the Hopi (Costello, 1997).

Those of us committed to teaching in public schools are coming to the belated realization that in respect of school reforms we should have been more like the Hopi Indians and remained true to our instincts and educative ideals. Somehow we lost our nerve and moral fiber at precisely the time when it counted the most. Instead of being indignant and vociferously denouncing recent changes to schools and teaching deriving from an ill-founded economic experiment, we mistakenly believed that if we ignored it for long enough then it would eventually go away. We were tragically wrong, and the consequence has been that our schools and other social institutions have been vandalized almost beyond redemption by those who argue that schools should be the engines for the economic restoration of sagging international competitiveness. We were too readily seduced by glittering prizes on offer from the fiscal snake-oil salesmen—quality, excellence, lean organizations, worlds' best practice, user-pays, multi-skilled workforce—all in the interests of international competitiveness. The realization that change can be for the worse, has been slow to catch up with us, in a context where change is naturalized and few questions are ever asked about "to what valued social ends"? Schools around the world have been co-opted into the bold new experiment of micro-economic reform, variously described as economic fundamentalism, economic rationalism, or simply the New Right ideology, with barely a thought about what is being lost and expunged ... The shrinking of the "imaginative space" (Zaidi, 1996) that has accompanied this single-minded pursuit of the "ruthless economy" (Head, 1996) has been matched only by the speed by which the shots are being called further and further away from what transpires in classrooms.

The educational policy experiment embarked upon around the world over the past decade of redrawing the boundaries around teaching through educational reform and restructuring, is in deep and possible terminal trouble. Teachers are reeling from the effects of poorly conceptualized reform policies that have literally torn the heart out of their work (Smyth & Shacklock, 1998, pp. 1–2).

To parlay for a few more moments with some of the points alluded to above. The situation just described is one in which teachers in all affluent countries have been consistently, willfully and systematically excluded from any involvement in reforms relating to teaching over the past three decades, except as docile and dutiful operatives in the final implementation stage of an agenda conceived and developed a long way from schools and classrooms. By any measure, this is a ridiculous and ludicrous situation. Quite why we would go along with a situation that consistently perpetuates such a demeaning view of a valued occupational group, almost defies explanation—that is, until we dig a little deeper into the distorted and diseased logic behind it that goes something like this:

- Teachers are 'interested' educational players in the sense that they know intimately what transpires in classrooms and schools, and they have a decided 'interest' in ensuring things work for them and their students—which may be quite different from what might be considered the 'national' or the 'economic' interest. For that reason, teachers are not to be trusted—they must be controlled, managed, and taught their place in the system.
- One thing that policy makers have to be seen to be doing is acting in 'can do' ways—that is to say, they have to demonstrate that they appear to know what the issues are, the complexities, what is going on, and furthermore, that they have a repertoire of 'solutions' to apply to dysfunctional situations, regardless of whether the purported solution is to the correct problem, or irrespective of whether they even understand any problem.

- What is paramount, is 'being seen to be doing', and that is what gets them into and keeps them in elected office.
- Something to be strenuously avoided at all costs by policy makers is to allow any outbreak of genuine democracy, for to do that would be to create the conditions that undermine their sole rationale for existence—being omnipotent and 'all knowing creatures'.
- The way to regulate and steer such an unwieldy social creature like schooling that is riven with so many contradictions, is through the unilateral proclamation of deliverable performance targets, devising programmatic solutions that are mandated, prescribing punishments (usually fiscal) for non-delivery, and allowing the 'hidden' forces of the market to sort out the regulative mess though processes like school choice.
- In a context of social Darwinism like this, schools that are the fittest (i.e., the ones where the parent clientele most closely matches the middle class norms of the school) survive and thrive, and through a process of separation by triage, the most salvageable schools will be provided with modest support to struggle over the line, and the rest will be allowed to perish or wither—all the while, with the finger of blame pointed at students, parents, and communities as being the 'cause' of their own predicament because of unwise lifestyles or inappropriate 'choices' (meaning indolence, and its attendant poverty).

When we pull out the pieces of the ideology and put it like this, it really does sound fanciful and ridiculous in the extreme—but we have only parodied the situation slightly.

What we have been talking about so far is the macro-political picture of the way in which the ideology of neoliberalism has been let loose and unremittingly inflicted on schools. It is clear that teachers have been actively excluded except in the most demeaning ways as compliant operatives, and parents have only been countenanced because of the pivotal role they play in exercising consumer sovereignty. Young people have been totally silenced and relegated to the most subservient position of all in this whole unhappy scheme we have all become caught up in.

How all of this impacts young people

It is important to say at the outset, that in our analysis we do not subscribe in any way to constructing young people as some kind of hapless 'victims'—far from it, we regard them as very active agents in constructing lives for themselves even though the larger frames within which they have to do this are not of their own choosing or making. It is certainly true that neoliberalism is leaving an indelible imprint on all of our lives in the way it fosters an emphasis on individualizing responsibility and constructing everyone as autonomous self-seeking 'enterprises' within the highly contestable presumption of *homo economicus*. Certainly young people are adversely affected by such a limiting view of human nature, but more importantly, they are actively engaged in a much richer and more complex process of identity formation than is suggested by this one-dimensional simplistic and highly misleading view of human beings.

The question to be put now, is how does neoliberalism evoke responses from young people (and schools), and in particular, how does it position them in relation to their experience of schooling? There are several lines of argument here:

- A focus in individualism through meritocracy, achievement performance, high stakes testing and the like, while seemingly rational from an adult perspective—is in marked contradistinction to the highly social and relational way young people conceive of themselves. Evidence of this is readily adduced if one asks a young person why they attend school, and the universal response is almost never 'to achieve higher test results'. The answer is invariably framed around sociability with their peers.
- The move by governments to force schools to be more overtly vocational in their course and curriculum offerings to make young people 'more job ready', while well-meaning, invariably backfires either because of inappropriate timing for young people who have yet to properly formulate a possible career path for themselves, or simply ill-informed as to the real aspirations of young people. It looks good politically to have young people transiting to employment, but it is a deal more complicated than that.
- The sorting and sifting of young people that is the inevitable outcome of the rankings that come with testing regimes, results in some young people being forced into pathways from which there is no way back—and here we are referring in particular to the tendency to corral working class kids into curriculum areas that can only lead them into low-skill, low-paid, insecure, work.
- The press to make schools appear as 'tidy' places for discerning consumers (which is what school choice really is), often means this occurs at the expense of schools wanting to divest themselves of those young people who are the most 'untidy' in all kinds of ways, (most notably, in terms of their behavior), and who don't fit at all neatly into schools. After all, who wants to be a consumer in an untidy school, metaphorically speaking?

To pursue the richer, more informed, and much more nuanced view of young people in their engagement with (or without) schooling, we need to heed the still largely unembraced call made by Postman (1979) over three decades ago, that we have 'an insufficient understanding of the complexity of the school as a social institution' (p. 8). Postman argued then, and the stakes are immeasurably higher now, that we are paying an incredibly high price in having 'parents, publishers, politicians, labor unions, state requirements, administrative convenience [and, we might add, big business, commerce and wealthy philanthropy]—each mak[ing] its demands and exact[ing] its price' (p. 8). Putting it most directly, he said:

> The classroom is not a place of simple teacher-student interaction—not even when the teacher closes the door. It is a place in which the claims of the various political, social, and economic interests are negotiated. The classroom is both a symbol and a product of deadly serious cultural bargaining (Postman, 1979, p. 8).

The long, and not so glorious, history of school reform, is littered with the results of the mindless intrusion of these various groups into schools and classrooms, and this intervention has been at the very considerable expense of silencing and riding over what ought to be the most important 'point of entry [of all]...the real life experience [and aspirations] of children in school' (Postman, 1979, p. 7). The consequence of this wanton exclusion, are on display for all to see, where:

> ...the experience of schooling [is one] characterized by boredom, confusion, and fear. Especially fear. Fear of not having the right answer, fear of not understanding things the way everyone else does, fear of being singled out, fear of not being singled out, fear of reproach, of ridicule, of failure. For many children the school is a House of Fear, no matter how charming its architecture, or open its halls, or contemporary its materials (p. 6).

To not put too fine a point on it, for those groups who have been pushed to the margins at the lower end of the social gradient, schools constitute 'a catalogue of damages inflicted by [what is quintessentially] a typical middle-class system of schooling', in which the effects are nothing short of 'intellectual and emotional carnage' (p. 6).

To back-track slightly for a moment, and to put some context around this. Postman (1979) argues that there was, in living memory, a brief period after the Vietnam War, in which there was a moment of enthusiasm for radical school reform in which 'the energy and fury of the educational reform movement [not to be confused with its look-alike that followed it] was a spillover from the antiwar movement' (p. 8). Postman, was referring, of course, to 'tough, reality oriented critics' (p. 7) like Kohl, Kozol, Hentoff, Herndon, Dennison, Silberman, to mention a few. But this flirtation with how schools might be better places for young people was to be short-lived:

> ...suddenly, it was over. Like a summer cloudburst that catches everyone unawares, does its sound and fury, and leaves no trace of itself. In this case, not even a rainbow left behind; only a dull, leaden sky (p. 7).

Perhaps as he says, the unrealistic 'Rousseauian glass' through which these radical reformers were looking, had sutured within it, the 'self-righteous' seeds of its own demise:

> Typically a school was imagined to be a place of obtuse, malignant adults who were dedicated to oppressing pure-hearted, liberty-seeking, instinctively humane children. With such cartoon imagery as this, it is no wonder so little was accomplished and that it ended so soon (p. 9).

What then, are we to make of all this in re-thinking schooling around young people?

We are certainly not the first to pose this kind of question, nor are we likely to be the last, but the fact that we have to do so is indicative of a lack of progress into what is an intractable issue and a dark pessimism that continues to surround it. We happen to think that Postman's (1979) contribution to this debate has been seriously under-valued, and that he was onto something really significant in his *Teaching as a Conserving Activity*. His argument that teaching is a 'conserving activity' is most intriguing. Essentially, he presents the not entirely novel view that intellectual and cultural advances are made 'not through argument but through argument and counterargument', and that 'counterargument' is crucial because of the way it 'makes the deficiencies of argument visible and makes improvement and synthesis possible' (p. 19). In other words, counterargument is necessary because without it 'there is no way to govern error, excess, or distortion; there is nothing for an argument to measure itself against or limit itself by' (p. 19).

Where Postman's (1979) argument is heading is in the direction of positing the view that cultures have embedded within them a kind of 'oppositional complementarity'—or in his metaphor, 'a thermostat, a mechanism for triggering opposing forces' (p. 19). In essence, 'a thermostat...releases a counterargument.. [and] the function of education is always to offer the counterargument, the other side of the picture' (p. 19). In this thermostatic view *'Education is best conceived of as a thermostatic activity'* (p. 19 his emphases)— that is to say, a way of interrupting the status quo and deploying oppositional ideas to keep a culture in 'working order' so that it does not become complacent, smug, and bogged down with a sense of its own self-importance.

Clearly, there are two sides to this: first, when there is volatility and rapid change, as we are experiencing at the moment, the function of schools is to act as a bulwark, a kind of institutional memory of more stable and certain times—hence we often hear the rallying cry of the need to 'return to the basics'; second, in situations of relative social stability, as we experienced in the long post-WWII period, 'the conserving function of school is...redundant...even dangerous' (p. 21). Herein lies the nub of the quite contradictory role of schools, both how 'to help conserve that which is necessary to a humane survival', as well as counteracting what is 'threatened by a furious and exhausting culture' (p. 25). This left Postman (1979) with three intriguing questions, which we have sympathetically re-framed for our purposes:

1. What do we need to do to ensure that young people are not left with 'incompetent intellects and distorted personalities'?
2. To what extent are schools and formal education up to it 'and competent to deal with' this task?
3. How may the education provided to young people 'oppose both emphatically and constructively' what is happening to our wider societies, and are schools capable of addressing these wider incursions? (p. 25).

These questions pose some interesting challenges in a context in which it is by no means certain that schools either have the will, imagination, or the capacity to challenge the situation that has put them in this situation in the first place. This seems to be a variant of what the postcolonial theorists have named as the Northern mainstream metropolitan views of schooling and what constitutes knowledge, willfully excluding indigenous forms of knowledge and its production. In other words, pushing young people to the exclusionary margins, is yet another instance of what Hickling-Hudson (2009) refers to as 'the imperializing capacity of knowledge production in the Northern metropolis'—in this case, the forms of school effectiveness, teacher effectiveness and evidence-based knowledge being warehoused by the World Bank, the IMF and the OECD—that is ricocheting around the world and being absorbed through processes of policy transfer.

Postman (1979) provides us with a very helpful orienting framework around which to 'trouble' what is happening in respect of young people, around:

- educational approaches that don't damage the identities of young people or warp their personalities;
- schools that understand young people and that give them 'voice' and 'agency';
- an education for young people that equips them to be critical of the world...and change it!

It seems that this constellation of terms with their focus on: undamaging, removing distortion, understanding young lives, giving voice and agency, and fostering criticality and change—are a powerful amalgam around which to capture what is happening to young lives, and what needs to be done differently. To put it most directly, what we are dealing with here is how education 'makes space' (Thiem, 2009, p. 168) and concomitantly, how schools can also alienate and exclude—but just before we do that we need to scope out some of the wider context around young people.

Geographies of exclusion... in the lives of young people

We want to situate the issue of young people's exclusion and alienation from school within the somewhat broader context of the increasing loss of public space that is coming to accompany various forms of overt and covet privatization of our lives. Controversies around alternative forms of social learning in neighborhoods and communities with/for young people need to lie at the core of any attempt at reclamation. Our argument is that we need to go considerably beyond the hermetically sealed view that the education of young people goes on only in schools and classrooms. Unless we look at where education sits in young people's lives in the neighborhoods and communities in which they live, then we will continue to come up with 'solutions' and 'treatments' that created the 'problems' in the first place.

Sibley's (1995) notion of 'geographies of exclusion' is a useful category from which to begin a consideration of 'the constitution of social space according to which some groups or peoples are deemed not to belong' (p. 49). That such groups are seen as threatening has 'long been used to order society internally and to demarcate the boundaries of society' (Sibley, 1995, p. 49). Indeed, the way Sibley (1995) sees it is that boundaries are constructed and policed in ways that are often emotionally 'charged and energized' (p. 46). Sibley (1995) argues that 'space is implicated in many cases of social exclusion' (p. 46), and the spatialization of boundaries is a technology for positioning young people, especially in the way they are treated in schools, as well as in other aspects of their lives.

While the term 'exclusion' has come in for criticism in relation to social and public policy because it has become 'a kind of vague catch-all used to describe a variety of societal inequalities and maladies' (Vanderbeck & Dunkley, 2004, p. 178), and in some quarters as a 'codeword for "poverty" or "material deprivation"' (p. 178), there are broader meanings that attach to it that include 'not only low material means but the inability to participate effectively in economic, social, and cultural life...' (Duffy, 1995, cited in Vanderbeck & Dunkley, 2004, p. 178).

Social geographers have been arguing for some time that the liberalization of Western societies with their focus on individualization and commodification is producing a situation of increasing Wrigley (2007) put it rather colorfully in terms of the following analogy:

> We are living through a cultural equivalent of the economic dispossession brought about by the enclosure of the common land (England) and the highland clearances (Scotland) (pp. 3–4).

To expand on Wrigley's point, young people and their parents, are being dispossessed and increasingly herded away from what C.W. Mills (1970) called a consideration of 'public issues' that are shaped and formed by social structures, towards reframing them as 'private troubles' (p.14) which we are led to believe derive from personal shortcomings and failings that have to be endured, borne and resolved by the individual. For Wrigley (2007), the paradox is that we are increasingly living lives that are 'high-pressured' but in what amount to 'disengaged ways' (p. 4), evacuated of relational meaning and replaced instead by synthetic and commodified exchanges. He invokes Albert Camus' (1948) description in *The Plague* around what life was like in France under fascist occupation, characterized as being 'frenetic and absent' (p. 4). What Wrigley seems to be alluding to is the way in which we are experiencing a huge case of deflection of attention away from the real issues occurring around us, which amount to an increasingly fragmented and unequal society, and instead, focusing on situations in which blame is directed towards individuals who are portrayed as being inadequate, deviant and in need of rehabilitation.

By way of illustration, in navigating a pathway for themselves into the 'skills economy' and its accompanying shrill rhetoric, Wrigley (2007) points to:

> the supposed need for everyone to become 'highly skilled problem solvers', [yet] most young people entering the labor market are confronted with a demand deficit rather than a skills deficit—there is simply not enough demand for their labor irrespective of skills levels (p. 4).

The result as Wrigley says, is that 'young people are confronted with an increasingly abusive tirade from politicians, inculcating a sense of worthlessness if they do not concur with this culture of instrumentalism' (p. 4). In poor areas of Britain, and we might argue in similar 'disadvantaged' parts of other so-called affluent countries, more and more young people are 'being criminalized, in the double sense of facing incarceration and of being labeled as criminally deviant' (p. 4).

One of the major ways in which young people are being excluded in this rush to privatize everything is through the increasingly 'passive participation' inflicted upon them through performative approaches to schooling—testing and account-

...bility regimes, compliance with disciplinary requirements around punctuality, dress codes and deportment (in marked contrast to how young people are actually living their lives out outside of school), and the general trend of schools in being obsessed with portraying themselves in a presentable light in order to garner 'market share'.

We don't want our views here to be interpreted as arguing for the loss of some 'golden era' in which young people had unfettered freedom, and where their views were listened to and respected—that was never the case. It is true that young people today have far more freedom of movement, expression and opportunities than almost any generation before them, but in social institutions like schools, and in the public and political imagination and media representations of them, young people are pilloried, constrained, controlled, exploited, castigated and manacled in unprecedented ways.

Young lives are also riven with paradoxes and contradictions. As Morrow (2005) found in her study of young people, the spaces for 'participation' (whatever that means) and invitations to young people to 'contribute to their communities' often amounted to being 'patronizing because in many ways young people were already contributing albeit in ways that were 'invisible' or not measured (p. 57). Morrow also found that in some cases young people had 'more say' within their families, and that when given participative opportunities in schools they were tokenistic at best. In the words of one young person, 'it's like they are trying to make it look as though we've got some power, but we haven't' (p. 62). For many of the young people in Morrow's (2005) study, schools were crucial 'as a site of social interaction' (p. 63), and they acknowledged the importance of 'the acquisition of educational qualifications'—but they were also places of condescension, where they were taught their place in the authority structure, and where their knowledge, aspirations and life experiences were not valued, and bullying and harassment were ignored or condoned. This led Morrow (2005) to conclude:

> we need to see active participation in the context of relationships within school in general. The quality of these relationships is likely to affect the extent to which children are likely to 'participate' (p. 64).

The story around the participation of young people in communities was not a lot more optimistic. Some of the comments from the young people in Morrow's study give a flavor of this. Leisure activities were noted as having been 'increasingly privatized' and of young people not having the money to participate, with the result that '"hanging about" outside is often the only activity available that does not involve spending money' (p. 65). When facilities are provided by governments of one kind or another, they are often inappropriate, as one young person put it: 'They just do things like little tiny parks for little kids...we don't want little parks'

(p. 65). This led Morrow (2005) to sum up her study thus: '...participation in terms of being actively involved in decisions that affect them in their neighborhoods, appears to be virtually non-existent for these children' (p. 65).

Much of this points to the systemic and structural issue beyond tokenistic involvement of young people, in which there are 'no consistent, formal channels though which to communicate or convert their energy into a positive resource for their neighborhoods' (p. 65). What seems to be missing from the official analysis by governments is any sense of the ways in which young people are constrained within their existing structures and settings...and how these constraints may affect their willingness to participate...'(p. 67). There is a desire on the part of authorities for young people to participate but 'only on the government's terms' with the young people being portrayed both 'as the problem to be solved, and as the solution to the problem' (p. 67). Morrow (2005, p. 67), leaves the most damning indictment and ultimate indignity until last, in citing from Ennew (2000), in pointing to what is being required of 'disadvantaged' communities:

> It is not fair to expect the powerless to assume responsibility for transforming the hierarchical structures in which their lack of power is inscribed. Indeed, to do this, is to blame them for their situation, and reproduces the same inequalities in political and economic structures that produce and maintain inequalities. In this respect, participation is a kind of conjuring trick (p. 5).

If we are going to interrupt the narratives of exclusion described so far, we will have to start in a very different place to that of denigration, zero tolerance, moral panic and criminalization of young people. To borrow from Vanderbeck and Dunkley (2004), it will necessitate a serious study of 'geographies of exclusion, inclusion and belonging in young lives'. It would need to commence by acknowledging that in some respects young people are treated by the wider society as 'transgressive' and excluded in the sense that they are often seen as occupying public spaces 'claimed by the dominant groups in society, or the threat that they will move into those spaces, [and thus] render[ing] them discrepant and polluting' (Sibley, 1998, p. 94). What is being contested here is the 'fixed' versus the 'fluid' conception of space, in which a more 'sedentary' or fixed view is challenged by a more 'mobile' or 'nomadic' view of space—and young people often fit in the latter. It is nevertheless also the case as Vanderbeck and Dunkley (2004) argue that we need to avoid putting a victim construction on young people because they are 'active cultural producers in their own right, capable of challenging exclusionary discourses and practices and creating their own complex systems of inclusion and belonging' (p. 177).

When applied to young people's lives, geographies of exclusion can take various forms, including explicit forms like 'ghettoization' based on race or ethnicity

(Vanderbeck & Dunkley, 2004, p. 178), homeless or 'street people' (Sibley, 1998, p. 94) who are considered to be 'a cause of discomfort and anxiety to politicians and others…[and thus requiring] regulation because they are in the wrong place' (p. 94). This 'transgressive' view, in which young people are placed at the margins, has two aspects to it. First, 'the fears and anxieties [young people] engender in the rest of the population', and second, the way in which they are 'trying to create spaces for themselves, to assert some degree of autonomy' (Sibley, 1998, p. 94). When young people are excluded from more than full participation in society what this does is 'serve to naturalize adult authority' (Vanderbeck & Dunkley, 2004, p. 177). We can also see the exclusion and further 'peripheralizing of young people's experiences and perspectives', operating on young lives 'in the field of knowledge production, when certain ways of understanding…are privileged over others' (Vanderbeck & Dunkley, 2004, p. 178). To invoke an example we will discuss in some detail later, young people can experience cultural exclusion in their school lives when they 'are steered towards particular training and educational opportunities' (p. 178), usually of a manual, semi-skilled or vocational kind, based on the social class they come from and the neighborhoods they live in, and are excluded from other more abstract forms of knowledge and academic opportunities that come with them.

Unsettling dominant 'deficit' and 'at risk' view of disengagement from learning and schooling

There is a significant and powerful body of literature (Swadener, 1990), supported by a very substantial consultancy and recuperative industry, that positions the issue of disengagement from learning and schooling as being connected to 'vulnerable' or 'at risk' categories of young people, with associated 'causation' being located primarily in the realm of individual 'victim blaming' (see Valencia, 2010, pp. 101–125 for discussion). The arguments are framed around the propositions that becoming disconnected from school is the result of low familial aspiration and success in education, often inter-generational; it is linked to poor parenting practices; that there is an enduring lack of commitment and self-discipline on the part of young people themselves; and that there is a consequent need for schools to ramp up more muscular policies to enforce compliance among recalcitrant young people.

There is a wider and more expansive public policy, media, and common sense imagination around the 'deficit' and 'at-risk' nomenclature that seems to be uncontestable and unassailable—and this is a perspective that deserves to be punctured and robustly contested. For starters, the point needs to be made that these are socially 'constructed' categories—that is to say, they are not natural or immutable, and they exist and are sustained only as long as they derive legitimacy from people who are prepared to endorse them as being efficacious explanations of the way the world is. Put most directly, deficit views have currency only as long as people are prepared to endorse them.

It may be helpful here, to rehearse something of Richard Valencia's (1997) arguments about the origin and nature of deficit thinking, how it operates, and along the way, to then apply the lessons from this analysis more broadly to why young people, especially those from backgrounds that *put* (deliberate inflection) them at a disadvantage, find it difficult to relate to and remain connected to the institution of schooling. At its heart, Valencia (2010) argues, deficit thinking is an ideological version of 'social Darwinism', which is to say it endorses of view of social stratification that says:

> wealthier, brighter, and moral—compared to the poor, intellectually dull, and immoral [people]—attain their privileged position because of their alleged fitter genetic constitutions (p. 9).

Valencia (2010) proffers six useful orienting features or characteristics of deficit thinking, and we will take a little license in how we build on these.

Firstly, 'blaming the victim' (Ryan, 1976) approaches deflect attention away from complex explanations and instead situate them in seemingly easier-to-fix locations, that involve fixing up individuals rather than challenging or changing social structures. Valencia says that the reason explanations like this have such universal appeal is that they constitute a 'victim blaming' ideology that obeys what Nagge (1932) referred to as the 'law of parsimony'—which is to say, that 'of any possible number of explanations of an animal act the simplest possible explanation should be employed' (Nagge, 1932, p. 493). In other words, humans always prefer 'simple explanations over complex explanations' (Valencia, 2010, p. 8). The effects of such parsimonious and reductionist ways of thinking are insidious in the way they end up 'driv[ing] deficit thinking' to the exclusion of 'look[ing] for external attributions' of the way human behavior is—explanations that more correctly lie in the 'inequalities in the political economy of education and oppressive macro-politics and practices in education [that] are ignored...' (p. 9). Reductionist explanations lend themselves to simple solutions that inhere in shrill cries to 'fix the individual student' (p. 9).

Secondly, because of the displacement and deflection of explanations onto victims, while silencing them from having a voice, the effect is that those who are ascribed such responsibility for the state of affairs—in this case young people who disconnect, disengage and 'drop out' of school—effectively suffer 'oppression'.

That is to say, they are the recipients of 'the cruel and unjust use of authority and power to keep [them]...in their place' (Valencia, 2010, p. 9). It is a case, Valencia says, of 'the more powerful blam[ing] the innocent' (p. 8). In relation to disengagement from school, this means that 'the authorities' (policy makers, politicians, administrators, and unofficial meaning-makers in the media) are the monopolists of explanations, and students, who by definition are minors and are therefore considered incapable of formulating and articulating a view of what is going on or how things might be done differently. This is a view we roundly refute, with some powerful evidence, in chapter 4. As long as the problem (or the fault) can be quarantined low down in the educational food chain, then those most affected can be muzzled on the grounds that they are 'the problem', and solutions reside higher up with wiser and older minds. Effectively, this is a way of keeping the young in their subservient place. Official explanations become further enshrined in the form of policies, guidelines and frameworks that take on a mind of their own in further institutionalizing and oppressing students, who after all, are legally captives until the end of the compulsory years of schooling.

In the third instance, Valencia (2010) argues that scholarly and research rigor are frequently jettisoned in favor of 'pseudoscience', and the passion and righteousness of deficit thinkers predisposes them to present as research what is in reality 'sloppy research' and flawed (or possibly diseased) reasoning, that leads to 'unwarranted conclusions', and even worse, damaging education policy interventions. Illustrative for our purposes here is the controversial work of American educational entrepreneur Ruby Payne (2005) and her proselytizing 'culture of poverty' which she misleading masquerades as 'research' (see Smyth, Down & McInerney, 2010, pp. 19–24 for a summary of her critics). This is an especially toxic set of unsubstantiated ideas that has been picked up with enthusiasm by educational authorities in many parts of the world and taken as a purportedly valid explanation of poverty and what needs to be done educationally. It is an instance of where what is posited to be a '30 year, qualitative case study' (Valencia, 2010, p. 77) amounts to an unsubstantiated set of spurious claims that purport to understand people living in poverty, but which in reality, are no more than a demeaning, derogatory, and insulting set of stereotypes. As Valencia (2010) reveals, Payne's claims, again unsupported by evidence, positions young people from contexts of poverty as having an alleged absence of 'cognitive strategies' (Payne, 2005, p. 89), 'impaired verbal tools', 'impaired spatial orientation', 'lack of precision and accuracy in data gathering', and an 'inability to hold two objects or two sources inside the head while comparing and contrasting' (Payne, 2005, pp. 92–93). Valencia's (2010) inference is that Payne is arguing that these young people are uneducable by virtue of their inherent 'mental retardation' (p. 91).

Fourthly, Valencia (2010) argues that deficit thinking has a 'temporal' or ideological quality, in that 'the ideological and research climates of the time shape deficit thinking' (p. 13). From the vantage point of our project, an illustration of this lies in the well-embedded view of working-class vocationalism—the notion that working class kids get working class jobs (Willis, 1977; Brown, 1987), and that the kind of curriculum that flows from that is inferior 'applied' forms of learning that equip these kids for manual or semi-skilled jobs. This an ideology that is shaped, sustained and maintained by official statistics portraying 'disadvantaged' areas and a vocational divide that young people and their families often internalize and become complicit in maintaining, often inter-generationally. For example, the often self-proclaimed notion that we are 'hands-on people'.

Closely following on from the ideological nature of deficit thinking is Valencia's (2010) fifth point about 'educability', which takes form in our research along the academic/vocational divide and the kind of curriculum that flows from it. At core is the notion that only young people with parents from professional backgrounds can really aspire to undertake academic subjects in school that will lead them to elite occupations and highly paid jobs. In essence, it is the segregation of the 'concrete and practical' (p. 15) forms of learning from the abstract and academic—something that young people are adept at picking up from their family backgrounds and that is powerfully reinforced by schools. This separation becomes all the more potent for those people on whom schools have given up, or conversely, who have given up on schools—and who by some miracle have re-connected with learning. For these young people, the obstacles for them are very significant indeed because they have been repeatedly taught that they are 'collateral damage'.

Finally, Valencia (2010) argues that there is an inherent tension between 'heterodoxy' (unconventional or dissident views) and 'orthodoxy' (conventional or accepted views), and that spaces are continually being constructed in which anti-deficit views can be asserted. In the case of our research, heterodoxy takes expression in the ways in which young people who had been 'written off' by the dominant ideologies that portray them as 'at risk', and therefore, destined to fail, are able to reinvent themselves and make vibrant and viable identities in the interstices of educational and learning programs that make the attempt to understand them and to work within those understandings.

Some troubling questions and the need for courage

As we emerge from surveying what can only be described as the carnage of the neo-liberal assault on education over the past four decades, we are moved to ask some troubling questions about the future of education for young people—like:

- What kind of society are we creating?
- Who are schools working for?
- What are the consequences of continued educational inequality?
- Ultimately, is this situation sustainable?
- Are we in danger of losing a generation of young people?

These are questions we will spend the remainder of the book addressing, in some shape or form, through the lives and experiences of young people themselves. Just before we come to the stories of the young people in our research, it is salutary to remind ourselves that none of these damaging policy trajectories are immutable—they can be altered. In a recent highly publicized and passionate plea for a fundamental reconsideration of the direction underpinning the trajectory of current education policy, Diane Ravitch (2010), a former U.S. Assistant Secretary of Education, very publicly recanted and repudiated the whole panoply of neoliberal market ideas that she had once staunchly supported. Her explanation as to why—'I [lost] confidence in these reforms…[M]y views changed as I saw how these ideas were working out in reality' (p. 2). In other words, they failed the *reality test*. Invoking economist John Maynard Keynes, who when chastised by a colleague for reversing a set of views he previously had endorsed on economic policy, replied '"When the facts change, I change my mind. What do you do, sir?"' (p. 2). Far from this being seen as a sign of weakness, this is extremely courageous thinking. Ravitch admitted to having been seduced into 'seeing like a state'—in other words, 'looking at schools and teachers and students from an altitude of 20,000 feet and seeing them as objects to be moved around…' (p. 10). What she had been blinded by as a policy maker was any capacity to understand what was happening, why things were occurring, the importance of context, and the assumptions that lay behind things. In an uncanny and insightful confessional, Ravitch (2010) admits:

> There is something comforting about the belief that the invisible hand of the market, as Adam Smith called it, will bring improvements through some unknown force. In education, this belief in market forces lets us ordinary mortals off the hook, especially those who have not figured out how to improve low-performing schools or break through the lassitude of unmotivated teens (p. 11).

At the core of Ravitch's educational policy disenchantment, is the view that concentrating on 'redesign[ing] the management and structure of the school system and concentrat[ing] on incentives and sanctions', is at the very considerable expense of failing to deal with 'rancorous problems like how to teach reading…' (p. 11). Most tellingly, at the heart of Ravitch's call for a dramatic educational policy reversal, among other things, is the need for a 'coherent, explicit curriculum' that has 'plenty of opportunity for children to engage in activities and projects that make learning lively' (p. 13).

Having someone of Ravitch's stature who was a 'true believer' in market reform and who has so unceremoniously dumped the 'dark side', is heady stuff, and Ravitch (2010) sums up the hard lessons she learned in terms of a long litany of 'distractions, wrong turns, and lost opportunities' (p. 225). She says, *schools will not improve if*:

- we continually reorganize their structure and management without regard for their essential purpose (p. 225).
- officials intrude into pedagogical territory and make decisions that properly should be made by professional educators (p. 225).
- we continue to focus only on reading and mathematics while ignoring other studies (p. 226).
- we only value what tests measure (p. 226).
- we rely exclusively on tests as the means of deciding the fate of students, teachers, principals, and schools (p. 226).
- we continue to close neighborhood schools in the name of reform (p. 227).
- we entrust them to the magical powers of the market (p. 227).
- charter schools [academies or their equivalents] siphon away the most motivated students and their families in the poorest communities from the regular public schools (p. 227).
- we expect them to act like private, profit-seeking enterprises (p. 227).
- we continue to drive away experienced principals and replace them with neophytes who have taken a leadership training course but have little or no experience as teachers (p. 228).
- we blindly worship data (p. 228).
- we listen to those who say that money doesn't matter (p. 228).
- we ignore the disadvantages associated with poverty that affect children's ability to learn (p. 229).
- we use them as society's all-purpose punching bag, blaming them for the ills of the economy, the burdens imposed on children by poverty, the dysfunction of families, and the erosion of civility (p. 229).

This is a pretty comprehensive and damning recant from someone who was a true believer! But let's not leave the situation at the level of well-meaning albeit reformed adults. The views of the largely ignored young people, are far more important—or as Jane Nagle (2001) aptly put it in the title of her book, the *Voices from the Margins*. We turn to those voices in the next chapter.

Methodology section

CHAPTER 3

Hearing the Voices of Young People

Our Method and Approach

'This is going to get pretty messy'

It's around 10:00 a.m. on a sunny April morning, and we're having a coffee break between interviews with early school leavers. The setting is a neighborhood house—a ramshackle but homely place that has been turned into an alternative learning center for young people. The relative calm is broken when 12-year-old Jimmy is ushered into the room. Next on our schedule of interviews, he has just joined the re-entry program and is still finding his way with the group. He is agitated and boisterous. Something is bugging him. An accompanying teacher asks if he wants her to stay for a while. 'No,' he says emphatically, 'this is going to get pretty messy'. Indeed it does. Jimmy is bursting to tell us his story. For thirty minutes he vents his anger and frustration at his former school, his teachers, his class mates, his father and even his younger brother. His account is laced with colorful expressions and homophobic language. He talks about his fascination with death, horror films and violent computer games, about staying up all night drinking coffee, and getting into fights. But it's not all bad news. Jimmy reckons his teachers in the community house are okay. 'They don't yell at me', he says. At various times we are amazed, perturbed, amused and horrified with what he has to say about his life, his interests, aspirations and experiences of schooling. There's a stunned silence when Jimmy departs. Questions are racing through our minds. What are we to make of this angry young lad? Did he deliberately set out to shock us with his outrageous language and bizarre claims? Was he alerting us to disturbing aspects of his schooling and home life? How will he fit into this new learning environment? What does the future hold for him?

To borrow from Jimmy, voiced research is 'messy'. There is no telling where a conversation may lead when young people have the freedom and space to talk openly about their lives. Discussions can stall or head in directions that seem to have little bearing on the research focus. This lack of predictability can be very unnerving for researchers, but it can also lead to unexpected insights and understandings about social issues. This is especially so when interviewees, like Jimmy, come from marginalized groups whose views and perspectives have been routinely excluded or silenced by dominant discourses and structures. We believe that one of the reasons young people's stories are pushed into the background, ignored, erased, or given less attention than they deserve, is that researchers are either unprepared or ill-equipped to engage in the risk-taking necessary to yield up vibrant accounts of young lives. Despite the explanatory powers of narrative research, proponents still have to battle against the prevailing orthodoxy of 'scientific, evidence-based' research with its emphasis on control and treatment groups and measurable outcomes. In our view, it requires more than a little courage and resolve to step outside the policy regime's preferred model of science-based research which has helped marginalize critical qualitative research over the past decade (Denzin, 2008). A lamentable consequence of this 'hands-off' approach to social inquiry is that the views of young people—those most directly involved in schooling—are rarely sought. For the most part, young people like Jimmy remain silent witnesses to what happens in schools.

In this chapter we elaborate on the nature of our research craft—how we designed it, how we undertook it, the tensions and contradictions involved, and how we struggled to make sense of, and honorably represent, the material we collected from young people. Van Maanen (2011) suggests that ethnographic research involves 'three constitutive (and overlapping) tasks—fieldwork, headwork, and textwork' (p. 218). Taking a cue from these descriptors we will discuss our approach with reference to:

- the ethnographic interviews and research methods which enabled us to access and project the voices of young people
- the theoretical, philosophical and moral orientation of the study, best captured in the notion of advocacy research
- the strategies involved in making sense of the qualitative data and the selection of themes
- the portrait as a powerful textual means of representing young people's ideas and perspectives

However, before we do so we want to elaborate a little on the context of the study.

Something about the participants, their contexts, lives and circumstances

As explained in chapter 2, the research underpinning this book focuses primarily on the individual, situational, political and institutional factors that promote re-engagement with education amongst 'disadvantaged' young people living in rural and regional Australia. The context of the study is important. High school completion rates in rural communities (especially those categorized as 'disadvantaged') are well below the national average of 70% (Dusseldorp Skills Forum, 2007)—a situation which has serious implications for Australia's economic and social development, not to mention the future employment prospects and well-being of young people.

Our research was conducted in three regional centers of south eastern Australia, an area which covers approximately 50,000 square kilometers and supports a population of 216,000 people. In the following overview of the sites and re-entry programs, we have assigned pseudonyms to place names, schools and participants. Dominated by mining in the second half of the 19th century, the economy of the region now relies heavily on agriculture, pastoralism, tourism and service industries. With a population of 85,000 people, Federation City is a major service centre for the region and has many of the cultural, social and economic amenities associated with urban living. Approximately 200 kilometers west of Federation City, Merino Plains (population 14,000) is an important transport hub and service center for a prosperous agricultural district. Forty-five kilometers to the north east, the smaller settlement of Crystal Springs (population 3,000) has a diverse agricultural economy and is a popular tourist destination. In common with many regional economies, the manufacturing sector of the district has declined markedly over the past two decades resulting in high levels of unemployment and welfare dependency in working-class neighborhoods and some rural communities. Significant numbers of students fail to complete school to the compulsory leaving age of 16, and there are concerns about the lack of connection and engagement of young people with mainstream schools.

Re-entry programs approved and funded by the State education system and technical and further education providers offer education courses for 400 young people across the region. Students unable or unwilling to return to traditional forms of schooling are enrolled in local schools but undertake accredited courses in off-campus community centers or neighborhood houses. Following consultation with regional education administrators and school principals, we negotiated access to *Connexions* and *Beyond School* (Federation City), *Stepping Out* (Merino Plains), *Youth Pathways* (Crystal Springs) and satellite courses in applied learning delivered at the three urban centers. We will elaborate more fully on the features of these re-entry options in chapter 4 but suffice to say they emphasize personalized learning, small group instruction, flexible teaching/learning structures, community engagement, skills for social living, applied learning, and work place education.

Often disparaged as 'school drop-outs', 'youth-at-risk', 'troublemakers' and/or 'disengaged learners', the 100 students who participated in the study comprised 39 males and 61 females ranging in age from 12 to 23 years with the largest number in the age group from 15 to 17 years. (Refer to Appendix A for a statistical summary of the participants in each site.) They included 5 Indigenous students and 15 young mothers enrolled in specially tailored re-entry programs for young parents. The majority of the students came from low socioeconomic backgrounds. Many had led transitory lives having moved school to school across state borders and several had experience of homelessness. In the absence of parental support, some were cared for by grandparents or other family members. Amongst our participants were foster children, victims of domestic violence, students with serious (in some cases life-threatening) medical conditions, young people suffering from depression and acute anxiety, and several struggling with drug addiction. One young male had spent time in a youth detention center and several had a history of violent behavior. The majority of students lived in suburbs and towns, but a dozen or so lived on farms and had a close affiliation with the land. Quite a few were balancing studies with part-time work and/or family responsibilities.

Although most informants had 'dropped out', were eased out or pushed out, of high school, two came from a background of home schooling with little or no history of traditional schooling. Whilst some students described their home life in terms of fractured relationships and unhappy childhood memories, others spoke of supportive, caring parents and family members. Far from being 'out-of-control' teenagers the majority presented themselves as mature, thoughtful individuals who were eager to talk about their setbacks, achievements and dreams for the future. There were marked differences in the lives and circumstances of our informants, but they did share some common experiences and aspirations. Most had a deeply ingrained sense of failure associated with their years of schooling, yet they had made a decision to re-engage with education in the hope that the re-entry program could turn their lives around. To borrow from Olson (2009), having been 'wounded by school' they were now involved in a 'healing process' that they believed could restore their confidence and enable them to lead worthwhile and purposeful lives. Most had a sense of agency and a new-found belief in the relevance of education.

A second group of participants included 8 educators (teachers, managers and integration aides) involved in the re-entry programs and 14 people from the community whom we regarded as 'significant others' in the lives of young people. Although many in the latter category were not directly involved in the education of students, they did have a connection through their professional work in such areas as clinical psychology, maternal health care, youth services, community policing, social welfare and youth housing. In some instances they worked closely with schools and teachers in the provision of counseling services, teaching programs and staff development. Some had insider knowledge of the re-engagement programs and others were able to offer insights into the issues confronting young people and the range of community services available to them.

Listening with intent — ethnographic interviewing

> There is value in researchers and policy makers cultivating an ethnographic sensibility because it pays attention to the complexity of students' lives. (Bessant, 2007, p. 21)

The research we undertook involved a range of critical ethnographic methods including embedded interviews, purposeful conversations, dialectical theory building, voiced research from the data, and representation of data through portraiture. From the outset we attached a great deal of importance to the ethnographic interviews with young people. Walford (2009, p. 272) claims that one of the key elements of ethnographic research in education contexts is 'the high status given to the accounts of participants' perspectives and understandings' (p. 272). This does not always happen. All too often research into student engagement and school retention ignores or downplays the voices of the young people that have most to gain or lose from education policies and practices. Cultivating an ethnographic sensibility (Bessant, 2007) is crucial if we are to gain insider understandings of contemporary social problems. As Smyth (2006) argues:

> If the intent behind educational policy is to bring about genuine school improvement, then hearing from those most deeply and intimately affected must be accorded a high priority and this means acknowledging and elevating the importance of ethnographic studies of schooling. (p. 33)

How can we hope to understand why students from disadvantaged backgrounds leave school and negotiate a transition back to structured learning opportunities without hearing their stories? What sense does it make to redesign curriculum, pedagogies and school structures without first finding out from students about what works best for them?

Notwithstanding what insights educators, parents, community agencies and policy makers might bring to the research, we made a deliberate choice to hear first from young people enrolled in re-entry programs. Between March and June 2010 we conducted 79 individual interviews and 10 group interviews within three regional centers. The semi-structured interviews of 30–45 minutes duration took the form of 'purposeful conversations' (Burgess, 1988) guided by focus questions that were sufficiently open-ended to encourage extended participant responses. In particular, we wanted to hear from them about:

- why they had become disengaged from school
- what prompted them to resume schooling
- what their new learning environment was like
- what had been the biggest obstacles in returning to learning
- what support they had received
- how much control they now had over their learning
- what effects re-engaging with learning had on their view of themselves, their life chances, and connectedness to others.

Honoring the voices of participants is not always an easy task. It demands a certain degree of discipline and patience on the part of researchers to actively listen to people rather than bombarding them with questions or constantly interrupt their storylines. It means treating participants with respect, being open to their opinions and ideas, not imposing our interpretations on them and, above all, encouraging them to tell *their* story. Burgess (1988, p. 138) argues that interviews developed along conversational lines open up the possibility of rich and rewarding dialogues which are denied in the question- and answer-technique of conventionally framed approaches 'where interviewing is a scientific technique that is detached from the substantial and theoretical concerns of the investigator'. In our view, overly structured interviews tend to inhibit the development of educative dialogues because they do not readily accommodate discussion of issues and ideas beyond the agenda controlled by the investigator. Because they are constrained by asymmetrical and power-laden relationships, they often fail to acknowledge the situated knowledge of participants and the intellectual contributions which they might make to the study. In these circumstances participants are unlikely to give of themselves, and there is little possibility of generating the kind of dialogic relationship necessary for some critical engagement with the research issues.

Our approach to the interviews typically went along the following lines. We introduced ourselves to the participants, explained the purpose of our research, assured them of the confidentiality of what they had to say, and sought their permission to make an audio recording of the interview. Having discussed the ethical issues and formal procedures, we invited them to tell us their story. 'You might like to begin with your time at school', we suggested. 'What were the good and bad experiences? What has changed since you joined this re-entry program? What differences has it made to your life?' We tried to make the interviews as personable and non-confronting as possible by maintaining a relaxed conversational style where participants could express their thoughts free of reproach and value judgments on our part. Occasionally we prompted them to elaborate on matters that seemed especially pertinent to the research topics. From time to time we asked for clarification of ideas and posed additional questions to open up the conversation. We always concluded the interviews by thanking them for their contributions and wishing them well for the future. Where possible, the interviews were supplemented with observations of education activities involving the participants, including whole class instruction sessions and in situ conversations with students.

We also conducted 23 individual and group interviews of 45–60 minutes duration with educators and 'significant others' in Federation City and Merino Plains. Our conversations focused on the impact of these programs on the education, health and life chances of young people, the obstacles they had encountered, the extent of community support for their learning, and the policies needed to enhance further re-engagement of learning. Gaining access to the stories of young people, their teachers and supportive adults through ethnographic interviews opened up a gateway to a better awareness of the complexities, uncertainties and possibilities associated with young people's identities. Listening to their accounts reinforced our view of the need to take a stand against institutional abuse, unfair structures and discriminatory policies that stand in the way of young people achieving a fair go in the education stakes.

Positioning ourselves—advocacy research

As researchers, we align ourselves with a socially critical tradition that is animated by a desire to transform social conditions for the benefit of the least advantaged. Addressing a conference on educational inequality, Fitzgerald (2009) claimed that researchers need to 'afflict the comfortable' and agitate within their communities in order to secure the attention of those who hold the power. We do not resile from the social responsibility to speak out against the inequities and gross injustices that we see around us, but in a spirit of optimism and hope. we also endeavor to reveal something of a more socially just and equitable approach to schooling. We do this in large measure through critical ethnographic accounts of communities, schools and other institutions that are working to promote a more humane and ethically constituted agenda for change (Smyth & McInerney, 2007; Smyth, Angus, Down & McInerney, 2008; Smyth, Angus, Down & McInerney, 2009; Smyth, Down, & McInerney, 2010). Rejecting the positivist notions of 'objectivity' and 'value-free' research, we acknowledge that we are engaged in overtly political research that:

> [goes] beneath surface appearances, disrupts the status quo, and unsettles both neutrality and taken-for-granted assumptions by bringing to light underlying and obscure operations of power and control (Madison, 2005, p. 5).

Critically oriented work in education recognizes that 'culture and power are an indissoluble couplet in daily life' (Carspecken & Apple, 1992, p. 508). Although schools and education institutions generally have a degree of autonomy, education is intimately linked to social, economic and cultural processes beyond the immediate settings which are responsible for the inequitable distribution of benefits in society. As will become evident from our research, racism, sexism and other forms of oppression are deeply implicated in unequal schooling outcomes and unjust practices.

We agree with Madison (2005), that '[c]ritical ethnography begins with an ethical responsibility to address processes of unfairness or injustice within a particular *lived* domain' (p. 5). In this study the *lived* domain encompasses the lifeworld of the young people who have re-connected with education in a context of deep alienation and disaffection with schooling and (in many instances) oppressive social and economic lives. Beyond 'listening with intent' to what they have to say we also position ourselves as advocates, not only for those students whose lives have been gravely damaged or restricted by unjust structures and policies, but also for those educators and others working with them to improve their life chances. Because the young people in our study were largely powerless when it came to speaking back to the policy regimes, we saw that we had a moral responsibility to do so with them and on their behalf.

An advocate is variously described as 'a person who upholds or defends a cause', 'a person who intercedes on behalf of another', and 'a person who pleads his or her client's case in a court of law' (*Collins Concise Australian Dictionary*, 2001, p.

20). The latter notion of advocacy is well entrenched in the Westminster legal system where the practice of acting for, or on behalf of others, is common practice in civil and criminal law. A growing body of socially committed researchers also sees itself as having an advocacy role when it comes to representing the lives and experiences of oppressed groups and communities, including, women, the poor, indigenous people, ethnic minorities, and people with disabilities. Outstanding examples are to be found in Kozol's accounts of homeless families and the 'savage inequalities' confronting the urban poor in the United States (1992, 2006), Fine and Weis's (1998) collaborative research project which attempted to influence social policy to improve the lot of the poor in Jersey City and Buffalo in the United States and Lather's (1995) study of women living with HIV/AIDS which was presented as a multivalent text.

Elsewhere (Smyth & McInerney, 2011), we have described what we do as 'advocacy ethnography', an approach which we believe breaks new ground in social research that affirms the importance of human agency and local knowledge. Though not well described in the scholarly literature, elements of advocacy ethnography appear under the labels of critical ethnography (Anderson, 1989; Foley, 2002; Madison, 2005; Willis & Trondman, 2000), public ethnography (Bailey, 2008), activist research (Fine & Vanderslice, 1992), and research reciprocity (Hinson, 1999).

Advocacy research does not start from a position of neutrality, but as Griffiths (2009) explains it comes from a sense of social commitment to act on 'behalf of a person or group, with the intention of doing justice'. Griffiths distinguishes between (a) participatory and collaborative research that is *researching with* a particular set of people in order to represent them, and (b) research which is conducted on behalf of the interests of groups which might find it difficult to speak for themselves, that is, *researching for* them. Our stance was participatory to the extent that the young people were involved in identifying pressing issues of importance to them and their peers. These were incorporated into the research report chiefly through portraits. We want to make it clear that in acting as their advocates we did not view them simply as 'passive victims' in need of our intercession and help. Rather, we saw them as active agents who, when given the opportunity and encouragement, were more than capable of speaking on their own behalf.

In rejecting what traditional schooling had to offer and embarking on alternative education pathways many of the interviewees had demonstrated that they were socially competent and actively involved in the negotiation of their social worlds (Hutchby & Moran-Ellis, 1998). This is a crucial point. As Moore (1993) points out, policy categories like 'at-risk', 'disadvantaged' and 'targeted populations' are politically laden terms that reinforce deficit views of young people and encourage paternalistic responses. We are not arguing that disadvantage and oppression are not the experience of many young people. Clearly there are students who, in the words of one of our colleagues, have received 'the rough end of the pineapple', but they are not merely victims of unjust policies and practices. They do engage in acts of resistance. They do have positive aspirations for the future and a sense of agency. How different might it be if those who label them as being 'at-risk' could envision them as 'students of promise' (Swadener & Lubeck, 1995). Young people's narratives in this book do contain sad and depressing threads, but they are also woven with stories of resilience, hope and a conviction that they can make something worthwhile of their lives.

Our approach to advocacy research draws on an interpretive tradition that strives to provide rich accounts of the lives and experiences of people, their culture and communities. However, it attempts to move beyond narrow functionalist explications by framing and explaining research issues in terms of their wider social causation and effects. Trying to sustain interpretive and critical approaches is not without its tensions. On the one hand, we were conscious of the need to remain open to the ideas of young people and theoretical positions, yet on the other hand we recognized a need to keep the spotlight on power relations and the hegemonic forces that constrain their sense of agency when it comes to making decisions about re-engaging with learning. In searching for sociological and political explanations rather than apportioning individual blame or culpability, we align ourselves with the work of people like Valencia (1997; 2010) who speak of the need to confront and challenge the constructed myths and expose the fallacies implicit in 'deficit thinking' applied to particular social groups. Students themselves became our chief informants about the damaging impact of negative stereotyping and vicious rumors on their lives. They also gave us insights into the pedagogies and policies that can challenge deficit views of the potential and capabilities they had as young people in disadvantaged circumstances.

Making sense of it all: Bringing empirical research into conversation with critical social theory

Discussing the trend in education scholarship to separate theory and research, Anyon (2009) claims that 'neither data nor theory alone are adequate to the task of social explanation' (p. 2). Rather, 'they imbricate and instantiate one another, forming and informing each other as the inquiry process unfolds (p. 2). We share Goodman's (1998) view that the 'ability to vicariously experience informants lives is at the heart of the ethnographic adventure' (p. 60). Putting on hold pre-conceived ideas and being open to what participants have to say seems to us to be a vital part of social research. In our case, insider stories generated rich descriptions of the institutional features of schools, alternative education pathways for young people, and the influence of culture, social class, gender, and community-related factors on learning and youth identity. We grouped their responses around commonly recurring themes, for example:

- negative experience of schooling: harassment, intimidation, bullying, victimization, punishment, exclusion, suspension
- disengagement with learning: alienation, estrangement, disaffection, frustration, resistance, opposition, dropping out
- success and failure in school, community life and the workplace
- the positive elements of engagement in re-entry programs: relationships, bonding, care, respect, opportunities, becoming somebody, place-based learning
- vocationalism: work and school, youth and the labor market
- popular culture, media, 'chilling out', youth identity
- the impact of: poverty, social class, racism, sexism, pregnancy, depression, ill-health on young peoples' lives.

Whilst we have sought to honor the voices of the participants in the text largely through the medium of portraits, our analysis draws on critical social theory in making more explicit the links between young people's lives and the larger political, social and economic systems which help shape their experiences. Our analysis involves a critique of contemporary education policy and the institutions which have historically failed to provide more engaging education pathways and life opportunities for young people living in adverse circumstances. A sense of hope also informs our view of what is possible in turning around young lives. This is developed most fully in chapter 6 where we outline what kind of frameworks are needed to endorse, support, and maintain these crucial pedagogically affirming directions that are revealed in the narrative portraits.

Real young lives—the incredible power of portraiture

I'm 14 years old and I've been in the Beyond School program for a year. I was being bullied at school, mostly because of my size. One day I just had enough. A girl slapped me and I punched her and broke her nose. I went to another school where they called me the new girl. When I left there I missed a whole year of school. For most of the time I locked myself in the bedroom. My dad made a deal with me that if I go to school he would give me a job as his apprentice in the tattoo business. I like tattooing. Art's my favorite subject and I've wanted to do tattooing since I was about 8. I also want to work with kids, maybe at a day care center. This place is like paradise for me. The people here are bloody awesome. (Kristen: Extract from portrait)

We were drawn to the power of portraiture through the writings of Sarah Lawrence-Lightfoot. In her studies of the cultural and institutional elements that make for good schools, Lawrence-Lightfoot (1986) sought to 'create a narrative that bridged the realms of science and art [by] merging the systematic and careful description of good ethnography with the evocative resonance of fine literature' (Lawrence-Lightfoot, 2005, p. 6). Woven into her text were carefully crafted portraits developed from transcripts of interviews with teachers, students and school administrators. Lawrence-Lightfoot regards portraiture as the epitome of good social science research because it has a capacity 'to (re)present the research participant through the subjective, empathetic, and critical lens of the researcher' (Dixon, et al., 2005, p. 10). If we want to 'convey the authority, wisdom, and perspective of the subjects' (Lawrence-Lightfoot, 2005, p. 6), we need more detailed, descriptive and richer narratives that reveal more of the identity and interests of participants and researchers. We see this as a counterbalance to the deficit and pathologizing portrayals of young people that seem to characterize a good deal of social research. A narrative portrait is rather like a verbal picture that seeks to reveal, expose, and draw forth its subject (Green, 2006) so that the reader has a greater sense of 'being there' (Stake, 1998, p. 3). As illustrated in the extract from Kristen's portrait above, the portraiture method 'rejects flat, stereotypical explanations for school success or failure and depicts the multiple layers of contexts represented by events and people' (Chapman, 2005, p. 28). Like many of her peers, Kristen had an unhappy time at school but has new-found hope in the *Beyond School* (re-entry) program where the teachers, in her words, are 'bloody awesome'. Kristen has a unique story and a unique way of telling it. Portrayals of this kind add to the authenticity of research because they present young people's versions of events in a way that preserves, as much as possible, their natural speech rhythms, choice of words and colloquialisms. We believe that the direct, and sometimes colorful, language of informants is more likely to captivate the interest and imagination of the reader than the somewhat dullish tone of selected quotes from transcripts.

In addition to narrative portraits developed from individual interviews, we have also crafted dialogic portraits from two-way interviews and multivocal conversations. In the following example we can see the way in which the encounter provides some direction and structure to the conversation as well as space within which informants can shape it and put their inflection on it.

'People can be very nasty'

We begin our conversation by asking the girls to tell us how they came to join the *Young Parent Group* in *Connexions*.

> 'School was not a good experience for me', says Colleen. I found it hard so I went to the local School of Mines to study. I did some work experience there and then I fell pregnant and left. Someone told me about this teacher, Frank, who ran this program so I started coming. I've been here two and a half years now.' 'I'm new to this city', explains Brooke. 'School was good for me but I went to school in another part of Australia and year 11 here was like doing year 10 again and I didn't see the point. After I had my son the health nurse told me about Frank. The girls have encouraging things to say about the program but as young mums they have been on the receiving end of community prejudices. Colleen elaborates, 'I went into the group because it was a good idea to bring the children and do things together, like art and things. Frank helped me to complete a First Aid course and I'm studying Certificate 2 and 3 in hairdressing. It's hard being a young mother in a town like this, especially when you are on the bus—because you don't have a driver's license—and people look down on you. The worst experience I had was when a man about 60 said to me "You should have closed your legs". It was horrible. Other older mums on the bus said that wasn't very nice.' 'I've experienced this too', says Brooke. 'People can be very nasty.'

Crafting narrative is a discerning, deliberative, and creative process that 'requires a difficult (sometimes paradoxical) vigilance to empirical description *and* aesthetic expression and a careful scrutiny and modulation of voice' (Lawrence-Lightfoot, 2005, p. 10). It is also an inherently political process for there is never a single story to be told or a simple answer to the research questions. Ultimately, it is the researcher's perspective, experiences, and ideological beliefs that influence the construction of the portrait. The methodological and textual aspects of our approach to portraiture are discussed in detail in Smyth and McInerney (2011). Broadly speaking, there are four main moments: first, an initial reading of the transcript during which we gain a feel for the interviewees and emerging storylines; second, a more focused reading where we note the relevance of the interviewees' ideas and research issues and unique insights they might offer; third, we select the content, edit the transcripts and craft the portraits; fourth, we crystallize the storyline in the form of a vignette with an appropriate caption and brief commentary. Where possible we allow the portraits to speak for themselves and try to avoid lengthy commentaries and analysis of what interviewees have to say. However, as researchers and writers we also have a story to tell and must ultimately analyze and make sense of what informants have to say about the research issue. We do not claim that participants are the authors of the portraits. As researchers and writers we make decisions about the selection of content and storylines which we believe shed light on the research issue and engage the reader. Inevitably, this will result in some compromises. Portraits do not convey verbatim the words of our informants nor do they tell us all that they have to say. However, we do try to remain faithful to the participants' intentions, create a space for their ideas, and retain their vernacular language. We hope we maintain a reasonable balance between the voices of our informants and our own voices.

Closing remarks

In this chapter we have set out the major methodological features of the research which underpins this study, but just as importantly, we have made explicit the ideological orientation of our work. Weiss (1994) suggests that when it comes to writing about their informants, researchers have a tendency to position themselves as: (a) critics, (b) dispassionate listeners and reporters, or (c) advocates. Perhaps it is possible to straddle these categories but from our perspective, maintaining a disinterested stance when confronted with injustices is not an option, nor is it sufficient to fall back on the principle that research should do no harm to participants. It must do more than this. To take a stand with/for those most adversely affected by unfair practices and discriminatory policies is to recognize that research has a moral dimension that transcends technical goals and purposes.

Lather's (1986) notion of 'research as praxis' (p. 257) resonates with our conviction that research should not only aspire to generate new knowledge but should also contribute to an understanding of the ways in which we can work for a more just world. In promoting this view, we see ourselves as 'translators bearing witness' (Lather, 1995, p. 49) to the voices of our informants, especially those young people whose lives have been damaged by oppressive institutions, social structures, and policy regimes. We hope we do so in the following chapters by representing their accounts in ways that respect their integrity and judgment, affirm their sense of agency, and offer some vision of hope for the future.

CHAPTER 4

Becoming Re-connected

Storylines from the Fieldwork

Introduction

> This place [an out-of-school learning center] is like paradise for me. The people here are bloody awesome. I love it....I like it here because of the people. Unlike school they don't force you to do things and you can do things in your own time. I haven't done work for a year so I'm trying to get back into literacy and numeracy. My life has changed. Now instead of getting pressured I can just take as much time as I want. I'm in control of my learning (Kristen: Beyond School)

Much has been written about the reasons why students like Kristen become disconnected from school and what is needed to re-connect them. However, all too often diagnoses and policy fixes are based on simplistic, ill-informed and highly pathologized judgments by so-called education experts and policy-makers with little insider knowledge of the lives, aspirations and capacities of young people, especially those living in the most adverse circumstances. In the rush to mandate curriculum frameworks, impose stricter accountability standards on schools and legislate to compel students to remain at school until 16 (in some cases 17) years of age, governments have largely ignored the views of people whom schools are supposed to serve—students themselves. What do young people have to say about their experiences of schooling? What are their expectations and hopes of education? What do they tell us about the features of schools that most repel them? Conversely, how do they describe the conditions that switch them on? What role do their teachers play in reconnecting them to meaningful learning? These questions are rarely asked of young people— or if they are, they are given scant recognition in formulating policy—yet they are crucial to understanding how students learn, why some choose to abandon school, why conventional schools are not working for some students, and how we can make schools more relevant and (in Kristen's colorful language) 'bloody awesome' places for young people.

In many this respects this chapter is the heart and soul of the book because it foregrounds the voices of youth in regional Australian communities that have suffered most from the damaging impact of neo-liberalism and globalization policies on economic and social life. Here we reveal though portraiture and selected quotes from interviews with young people, something of what was happening in their lives as a consequence of their disconnection from mainstream schooling. More importantly, we show how they came to re-discover a passion for learning under a very different set of circumstances. In what follows, we shall describe a little of the archeology of the programs in community-based, flexible-learning centers and the dedication of people that helped to turn around their lives. We are under no illusions as to the difficulties and tensions involved in reconnecting disaffected youth to schooling. Many young people are wounded not only by the dehumanizing effects of educational institutions but by the oppressive (in some instances appalling) conditions under which they live out their lives. Poverty, homelessness, family trauma, sexual harassment, domestic violence, and racism intersect with and compound the degree of alienation and disadvantage that far too many students experience in school.

The 10 or so portraits we have chosen to include in this chapter from the 100 compiled in the research project reveal some very raw and sad accounts of young people, but equally there are incredibly courageous, optimistic and inspiring stories of success in working against the odds. Narratives of a reconstituted sense of worth and new-found agency from teenage mothers, dispirited adolescents—some on the brink of suicide—switched-off learners and neglected youth, testify to the transformative possibilities of education and to the inner strength and resolve of some of the most marginalized young people as they strive for a better life. Importantly, their stories challenge the negative stereotypes and deficit views of young people in disadvantaged circumstances that frequently abound in policy documents and community attitudes.

The chapter begins with an overview of re-engagement programs in the research sites—how they evolved, what they are attempting to do, what makes them different from mainstream schools and how they function. We then turn our attention to the discourses of school connectedness that influence policy and practices in tackling youth disengagement. Here we highlight the inadequacy of traditional approaches which seem more intent on preserving the status quo than challenging the hegemonic nature of secondary schooling. This is followed by an account of young people's re-connection with education around themes related to identity formation, relationships, supportive networks, and curriculum and pedagogy. Finally, we discuss the problematic issues associated with the flexible-learning options for these young people and the extent to which they have been able to deliver on their promises

Re-engagement with learning beyond the mainstream

As outlined in chapter 2, disengagement of young people with mainstream schooling is a widespread phenomenon but it is especially acute in rural and regional Australia where school retention rates are well below the national average. This is a problem for parents and caregivers because they have a legal obligation to ensure that their children attend school. It is also a major challenge for schools and education departments which have a responsibility to provide a relevant and engaging curriculum for *all* students in the compulsory years of schooling. It is a national concern because—as political leaders keep reminding us—governments cannot achieve economic and social goals without a well-educated and highly skilled workforce. Lastly, it is a problem for young people themselves who are not only disadvantaged in terms of employment opportunities but are unable to obtain a Youth Allowance unless they participate in either full-time (at least 25 hours a week) education, training or employment or a combination until age 17.

In the current policy context, state and regional education departments and schools have gradually come to accept the need for more flexiblility with relevant learning programs for so called 'at-risk' students. Typically, these take the form of specialized courses and targeted programs within schools or flexible learning options in out-of school settings (Department of Education and Early Childhood Development, 2010). Despite attempts to promote more learner-centered and community-engaged forms of learning, as exemplified in the notion of middle school pedagogy, few reforms have seriously threatened the hegemony of the traditional high school. It's as if the fault resides within the individual not the institution, hence alternative arrangements have to be made for those who do not fit the mould.

Our research was confined to community-based re-engagement programs in three regional centers of southern Australia. Approved and substantially funded by the state education system, they provided 'second chance' opportunities for young people unable or unwilling to return to normal forms of secondary schooling. What follows is a brief explanation of the programs.

Connexions

Established in 2005 as an alternative to the mainstream curriculum in Federation City High School, *Connexions* offers a range of education options for some 185 students in the secondary years of schooling. Referrals come from school authorities, health workers and community agencies, but in many instances students themselves are the best recruiting agents. Most of the instruction takes place in a state-of-the-art learning center where students have access to an information technology hub, multimedia center, professional recording studio and meeting rooms. Some courses are offered in Federation City West Community Center. With the support of teachers and counselors, students develop a personalized learning plan which guides their education pathways. Learning is structured around two literacy and numeracy appointments per week, and students can select from 35 electives that incorporate community-based studies, TAFE-accredited subjects, work experience and service learning. The majority of students participate in studies leading to a certificate in applied learning, but some choose more academic subjects of a high school certificate course that satisfies entry requirements for university. Assigned a small group of students, teachers are responsible for managing the curriculum, maintaining home and parent contact and negotiating electives and learning plans with students. A *Connexions* program catering to the needs of young parents operates from a neighborhood center.

Stepping Out

Approved by the state education system and supported by a consortium of regional service providers, *Stepping Out* was developed in 2006 to provide a more flexible learning-environment for disengaged students and early school leavers in Merino Plains. Students are enrolled in a local secondary school but the program operates off the school site in a converted (soon to be demolished) house near the town center. Each student attracts $6000 from the state government resulting in an annual income of $360,000. This has to pay for staff salaries, rent of premises ($200 per week), maintenance of home and gardens, and teaching resources. Approximately 60 students aged between 11 and 18 years are engaged in a curriculum which has an emphasis on life skills, literacy and numeracy, work-related studies and subjects which will enable them to complete their secondary school certificates. All students have an individual learning plan developed around their needs and interests. They have an opportunity to enroll in TAFE-accredited courses and participate in cooking classes, visual arts programs, recreational activities and self-development sessions. Classes are small—usually 4 to 5 students—and one-on-one support is available for students with special needs. Teachers see that they have a responsibility for the health and well-being of students and strive to connect them to their communities through work experience, local studies and volunteering programs. Counseling, health care and welfare support services are available to students. *Stepping Out* also has a specially designed program for young mothers and pregnant girls.

Youth Pathways

Youth Pathways is one of several education programs for young people operating out of a privately managed neighborhood house and learning center in Crystal Springs. Some of the students who join the program have been home-schooled and others have a history of disaffection and disengagement with mainstream schooling. All have individual learning programs, are able to combine part-time study with employment and family responsibilities, can pursue school certificate in applied learning or academic studies, and are able to access TAFE and other nationally accredited vocation and training courses.

Beyond School

Affiliated with Federation City West Community College, *Beyond School* commenced in 2000 as an education and training program for disengaged young people in the age bracket from 13 to 19 years. By comparison with the other re-engagement programs, a higher proportion of the enrolled students are in the upper primary years of schooling. A team of teachers and a counselor work with small groups of students in the areas of literacy, numeracy, personal development and self-esteem. A good deal of emphasis is attached to the acquisition of life skills and to hands-on, contextualized learning. Students participate in work experience programs and have access to IT training, automotive, woodwork and metal craft workshops, a well-equipped kitchen and recreational facilities. One of the accredited outcomes is a certificate of applied learning.

Satellite Applied Learning Certificate courses

Several schools in the region, including Federation City South High School, Crystal Springs High School and Merino Plains High School, have introduced community and/or satellite applied learning programs delivered off the school campus. In community programs 100 percent of the qualification is delivered by an external provider contracted by the school, whereas in a Satellite program the home school continues to deliver part or all of the qualification (Department of Education and Early Childhood Development, 2009). In common with other re-engagement programs that we observed, there is the emphasis on work-related studies, scope for negotiating topics for study, flexibility in the organization of the curriculum, a high level of teacher support for students and an emphasis on developing the sites as adult learning environments. Subject integration and learning in context seem to be the key features. Teamwork, collaborative learning and social skills are promoted through all of class activities such as camps, and field trips. Students are involved in certificate courses such as retail, building and construction, carpentry, automotive, delivered by TAFE and other providers. They include components of work experience, job preparation and the preparation of a personal portfolio.

In summary, whilst re-engagement programs at the sites differ in some respects, all aim to provide a qualitatively different teaching and learning environment to that which young people usually encounter in mainstream schooling. In many cases, individually tailored programs allow students to pursue education, employment and training options of interest and relevance to them. Flexible structures, programs and assessment practices accommodate individuals with special needs, family responsibilities and part-time work commitments. The relational aspects of learning are placed at the forefront as teachers work with students to reclaim agency, self esteem, and a positive sense of identity. To varying degrees, the programs take account of the socio-cultural experiences of young people and strive to make stronger connections between classroom learning and community life. In many instances, the centers support students through the provision of counseling programs, assistance with finding accommodation and financial resources, and help with child care. There are some problematic aspects arising from funding arrangements, management structures and curriculum options, but as we shall see from what students have to say, these programs have managed to turn around the lives of some very dispirited and unhappy young people.

Becoming re-connected to education

A recurring theme in young peoples' narratives is the sense of disconnection they feel from mainstream schools. Being valued, appreciated, supported and involved in their education is important to students, but many describe schools as uncaring places where they are treated unfairly and are presented with forms of learning that have little relevance to their lives and interests. The mismatch between what schools have to offer and what students are seeking from their education can lead to disaffection, disruptive behavior and ultimately to an early exit from school. This was Bev's experience.

> I never got along with the teachers [at high school]. They didn't like me and I didn't like them so they got rid of me. I was really disruptive. I went to school but didn't go to classes. The problem was the form of learning and the teachers. They'd tell you to do something but not explain it.' (Bev: Connexions)

Promoting school connectedness and a sense of belonging is often advocated as a means of engaging students like Bev, however the notion is usually described in rather individualistic and psychologistic terms as a protective strategy for 'at-risk youth'. The Wingspread Conference at the University of Minnesota (2004), which brought together a group of researchers and representatives from the education and health sectors, defined school connectedness as 'the belief by students that adults and peers in the school care about their learning as well as about them as individuals' (Blum, 2005, p. 16). Important as the idea of caring relationships may be, it is still a somewhat restrictive view of connectedness because it fails to acknowledge the broader context in which students learn. Connectedness, as Zyngier (2008) points out, 'implies a relationship between the home, school, and community, as well as between the curriculum and students' real life situations' (p. 1). One of the responses of educators to an apparent lack of connectedness to schooling of disaffected youth is to call for a far a more practical real-life curriculum. However, 'such a pedagogical approach doubly disadvantages the already disadvantaged students…by serving them up more of the basics and busy work instead of actively engaging their intelligence' (p. 1).

According to Zyngier (2008), it is possible to discern three discourses of school connectedness: a transmissive deficit notion which views the purposes of schooling largely in instrumental terms as preparation for the workforce; a constructivist and individualistic notion which appears somewhat benign in promoting the notion of equality of opportunity but which largely ignores the ways in which a hegemonic curriculum reproduces existing inequalities; and a critical, transformative and empowering notion which enables students to take more control of their lives, develop a knowledge of collective as well as individual rights and 'be connected to a more participatory social vision than that of providing the human capital needs of industry and business' (p. 6). At one level, connectedness may be promoted through a school culture which fosters a sense of belonging and an ethic of care for students and accords them a voice in school decision making. However, a more transformative approach seeks to incorporate young people's lives, cultures and experiences into the curriculum; link them to community resources, networks and organizations that can further their social, economic and cultural development; and create opportunities for them to contribute to society through service learning and involvement in community-building activities.

We are not suggesting that re-engagement with learning in the out-of-school research sites encompassed all the features of a transformative view of connectedness, but young people told us in no uncertain language that re-connection from their experience was radically different from disconnection. Informed by their views and perceptions, we have written our account around four overlapping themes which are depicted diagrammatically in Figure 4.1.

- *Becoming somebody—connecting to self*: Identity formation and the reclamation of agency and self-belief is possible when young people have greater control over their learning and are provided with skills, knowledge and resources that enable them to envisage more optimistic futures.

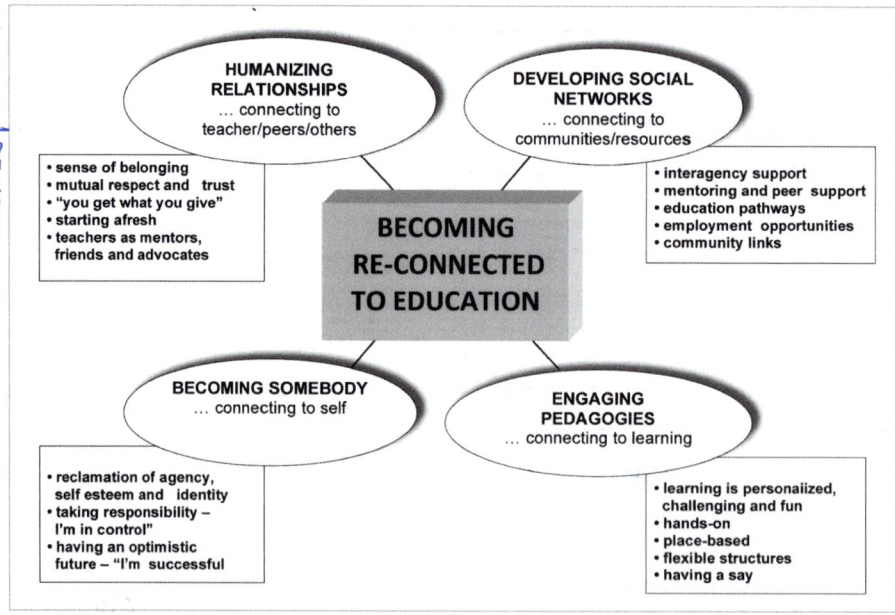

FIGURE 4.1: Becoming Re-connected to Education

- *Humanizing relationships—connecting to peers, teachers and others*: Building a sense of community, breaking down the institutional nature of schooling and establishing norms of care, trust, respect and supportive relationships is crucial to learning.
- *Developing social networks—connecting to communities, resources, and opportunities:* Building capabilities (Sen, 1999), youth networks and inter-agency services, mentoring and peer support programs is another fundamental imperative.
- *Engaging pedagogies—connecting to learning:* Engaging young people through personalized and challenging curriculum, valued education pathways, flexible-learning structures, community-based studies, and student voice is indispensable.

Becoming somebody: Connecting to self

The notion 'becoming somebody' (Wexler, 1992) is a way of thinking about the process of identity formation that stresses young people's capacities to make something worthwhile of their lives. It also draws attention to the socially constructed and incomplete nature of identity development. That is to say, 'becoming somebody' is always something in the making (Smyth et al., 2000). However, the extent to which individuals can act independently and exercise free choice in how they lead their lives is quite problematic. As White and Wyn (1998) point out, young people negotiate their own meanings, lives and futures in the context of specific socio-cultural, political and economic circumstances which may enhance and/or restrain personal agency. A desire for economic independence, for example, may be out of reach for many students. Writing about the crisis of youth in the United States, Giroux (1996) claims that many youth face an uncertain future in a declining economy that is likely to condemn vast numbers to the ranks of the unemployed or to low-skilled, poorly paid jobs. Navigating an entry into the Australian labor market, where youth unemployment exceeds 20% in some regions, is also fraught with difficulty for school leavers.

Notwithstanding the limits to self-actualization, the belief that schooling can support students to become more independent, resourceful and civic-minded individuals is surely one of the most important goals of education. However, an overriding view of disaffected students is that mainstream schools often suppress their identity and creativity by treating them as children and imposing unreasonable limits on their freedom and capacity for decision making. Rather than helping them to become more autonomous the institutional nature of high school life, embodied in petty rules, sanctions, routines and regulated activities, tends to crush the human spirit through an undue emphasis on compliance and conformity. For those students struggling with academic demands of schooling, feelings of inadequacy are often reinforced by deficit labels (e.g., 'at-risk' students), competitive assessment practices that consign them to categories of failure and an inhospitable learning environment. Now attending *Connexions*, Amanda describes how she was consigned to a 'run-a-muck' category at school:

> I never had good experiences with school. When I was 14 teachers were telling me to leave because they were going to kick me out anyway. They said they couldn't handle me for a full day so I was on half time. I sort of stayed there to spite them until I was 15 and I completed year 9. It wasn't bullying that caused me problems it was just the whole dynamic. I'm a bright girl and I'm good at English but the teachers just didn't care. They give the attention to the 'A' students but not to the 'run-a-mucks.'

Olson (2009) claims that students like Amanda are wounded by school. Amongst the many wounds inflicted on them are the wounds of compliance, the wounds that numb, the wounds of underestimation, the wounds of protectionism, and the wounds of the average. As a result students come to believe:

> they aren't "smart"...they don't have what it takes to succeed in school (and by implication, life)...all their efforts, no matter how hard they try, are below standard...their ideas lack value or validity...they are "flawed people"...they feel ashamed of themselves and their efforts...they show less pleasure, less courage in learning...have lowered ambitions, less self-discipline, and diminished persistence in the face of obstacles. (p. 26)

Reclamation of agency and self-belief

The wounds of schooling run deep but as we shall see from the following portrait, a more humane approach to education can assist students to reclaim a sense of agency and self-belief. Diagnosed (or perhaps misdiagnosed) as an attention deficit student in secondary school, Bernie joined the *Connexions* re-entry program in Federation City and gradually came to see how education might work to his material advantage.

Bernie's Story: 'If I stick my head down I can do whatever I want'

> I started year 7 at my local secondary college but I began to get more and more out of control. I got put on retalin and stuff for ADHD. I was not even allowed to set foot in the maths class

because I was disrupting the class. I wasn't getting any education. If I walked in they would just ask me to leave straight away. I reckon I spent more time in the vice principal's office than in the class. Then they assessed me and got me into Connexions. It's a more relaxed environment in which to learn and more kids want to come here because you can have a ten minute break when you want to. You're not stuck in the classroom, so it's good. They've helped me with a lot of things. I got a part in a film that was shot in a nearby town and went to an international film festival. I've now got an agent. I've done advertisements and a recording. All this has given me a lot of confidence and my studies have done well. I've been in Connexions for two or maybe three years now. When I first came here they didn't crack down much on students because the more they did the more kids would leave. Then they brought in the curriculum and more kids want to come here because you can get certificates. It's a bit more structured and that's a good thing because kids used to take advantage of the situation. Now it's their choice to come here. I've done certificate courses in hospitality and food handling and I have a red card so I'm permitted to go on building sites. I did a bricklaying thing for three months. They give you opportunities here. If you put your head down and work they'll do all they can to help you. If it wasn't for this program I wouldn't be in school at all. I don't know where I would be now. It's changed my life a lot. My mum's stuck by me and thinks the course is good. I have brothers and sisters but they live with my dad. I've met them a few times but don't have anything to do with them. I didn't have any ambitions at all when I came here. I didn't care where I ended up but now they give you options to turn your life around. If I stick my head down I can do whatever I want. If you give the teachers the time they will give you time. They are really good. When kids cause trouble the teachers stop it pretty straight away. Some of the kids who come here have a lot of anger issues but if you stop it straight away it's okay. I made the choice to come here. I'm hoping to get some work in films. Yeah it's good money. I got more parts but I dropped off because life got in the way. I'm not sure what I'll be doing in 2 years time—that's why I'm here. I might go and work in the mines because it's good money.

On the question of 'becoming somebody', Bernie has some instructive words to say about what he gained from *Connexions*. First, he acknowledges that there is a good deal of freedom and flexibility in this environment compared with school. There are rules and structures but he accepts that it's his choice to attend classes and he has to take responsibility for his own learning. Second, he can see the relevance of the courses on offer and how they might support his employment aspirations. Certificates of achievement reinforce his new-found conviction that he can succeed in school. Third, although getting a job is a high priority for Bernie, he has also found an outlet for his creative talents in the film industry. His participation in *Connexions* has imbued him with a greater degree of agency, hope, and self-belief in his own ability to make something of himself, both in terms of his desire for economic independence and cultural identity.

Projecting a sense of hope and possibility

Bernie's story reveals how a more enlightened approach to schooling can enable students to project a sense of hope and possibility about their futures. This also comes to the fore in the next portrait. Kicked out of school for being a 'disturbing influence' and seemingly directionless in life, Ben was on the verge of criminal activity that could well have ended in juvenile prison—a fate that had befallen his cousin. However, with the support of his teachers and an understanding employer he managed to turn his life around to the point where he too can envision a far more optimistic future for himself.

Ben's story: 'This place is a bit of a life saver for me'

I'm 16 years old and I've been in Stepping Out for a couple of years now. In year 7 I had no friends so I went out of my way being silly trying to make friends. I was disruptive and disrespectful. In year 8 I was asked politely to leave secondary school because I was a disturbing influence. I asked to go to Stepping Out and I enrolled there. I stopped going for a year and then returned before stopping once again. When my teacher asked me to do a work placement at a catering service it caused me to change my thinking. I had to learn how to relate to people in the workplace. I couldn't tell someone to go "beep". I have to show respect if I want respect back. This year I'm studying hospitality in VET at the TAFE because I want to become a chef. I've done my first aid course and my responsible serving of alcohol course. At the end of my work placement I had to make a speech about what I learned and how I enjoyed the catering place. Since that presentation mum and dad think that I can amount to something now instead of just being nothing. My health is improving and I enjoy going to the gym. If I wasn't coming to Stepping Out I'd probably be drinking and into drugs. More than likely I would be a 'juvie' (juvenile offender) like my cousin. The principal at the college told me about Stepping Out and I argued with mum about coming here because she said that only idiots come here. I tell them that they're wrong and they shouldn't throw their life away like I was doing. The teachers here are very understanding. They give you a few more chances and it's easier to work with smaller groups. I tried to get my cousin to come here but it was too late. He will probably get a few years in prison for the crime he committed. A lot of my friends from the college went into drugs and some got into vandalism and stuff. This place is a bit of a life saver for me. People try and give you advice but being a teenager you tend not to listen and then the police get involved and they start coming down on you and it doesn't feel very good. Here they try and figure you out and try to work the way you want to work. Then they will work your way. You come here and talk to the teachers and tell them what you like doing. The applied learning certificate course involved a lot of things. I do English instead of maths and I don't do any projects or anything. We got asked to do a garden and design things for the new Merino Plains gardens that are going to be built. I haven't done any planning yet. My cousin and another friend were going to do it but my cousin is put away and my other friend is pretty lazy now days. But it's going to be good. If I have kids I can tell them that I helped build that or helped design that. Since coming here I've grown up a lot. I've been finding out what life is about. If you die it's over basically. If you go down one path it's for the rest of your life. I'm in control of myself now. I have told people about my life but I've not gone back to the college. They won't even let me on the grounds. After I've done my two years here I am going to see if I can get an apprenticeship in Federation City. Now my aim is to finish a number of certificate courses and make a career out of cooking. I had to cook at the works expo—chips, potato cakes and all that stuff. There's nothing better than a career you enjoy doing—one that can take you all the way around the world. (Extract of a portrait developed from a transcript of an interview with Ben 22/4/2010)

One of Ben's most telling observations is that teachers in *Stepping Out* work with students rather than trying to impose their own solutions on them. 'Here they try and figure you out and try to work the way you want to work', he says. Ben feels that he has more power over his learning and can see a much closer connection between the curriculum and what he wants to do with his life. As with many of the students in his group, the drive for meaningful employment is a dominating factor in Ben's attitude to education, but in a sign of growing maturity he reveals a capacity to reflect on how he has changed as a person and where he is heading in life. From his perspective, the choice to re-connect with schooling is not just a smart move, it's a life-saving decision.

Being in control

A central theme in Ben's story is the ownership he has over his learning. Being able to choose courses of study that are relevant to his vocational aspirations and interests is a powerful motivation for remaining connected to education. He can now see the purpose in his studies because he has a say in what and how he learns. Many of the students we interviewed related similar stories. Robbie remarked: 'At high school you get work and you get told to do it. In *Beyond School* you control your learning.' Being able to express his own identity was a pressing issue for Thomas:

> At mainstream school no piercing and stuff was allowed. I just want to be my own person not who they tell me I should be. Here [in Connexions] you can be who you want to be. They treat you more equally—not so much as a child.'

What repels most students in formal education is their lack of institutional power. To a very large extent, 'curriculum is made for them by others' (Shor, 1996, p. 31) and students are required to submit to the authority of school rules and sanctions. However, as Jenny explains, students are likely to have much more control over their education in re-entry programs such as *Stepping Out*.

Jenny's story 'I like to be in control'

I'm 19 years of age and I've been in Stepping Out since it started in 2008. I was in year 9 when I stopped going to school. I was hanging around with the wrong crowd and got kicked out of home. I just couldn't get into the rhythm of school and eventually got kicked out. Then Stepping Out phoned me and asked me if I wanted to do a program with them. So I got in and I was on and off there for a bit because I was still hanging in with the wrong crowd. I just couldn't get out of bed. I wasn't capable of making proper decisions. I was really a mess. The problem was mainly at home. Stepping Out is different to school. For a start, it's not so strict which is good because I have a problem with rules. I can choose to come here or not but at school I had to go. There they said you have to do this and do that but here you can do it your way. Schools are too strict and boring. I'm a hands-on person so I don't like writing and that. Last year I did a massage course—learning where you put your hands and so on. It's easier to see how it's done rather than learning it from paper. It was good to see it on the sheet and then see it on the body. I wanted to be a massage therapist since I was 10 and it hasn't changed. I come to Stepping Out two days a week but I don't work at present. I'm a little bit scattered at the moment and I'm living with friends. I help out with the 5 year old daughter of the woman I'm staying with. There are rules here—courtesy, respect, manners and things like that—but I'm not treated like a brat child. I'm treated like a human being. I can see changes in myself. I'm more organized. I look at things differently and try to do things in different ways if something doesn't work out. When I was at school the teacher was in charge but now it's me. I like to be in control. One of the things I've done in this program is to work on a project that was put to me at the start of the year—a talking book or a radio show. I thought it was boring so I made my own track and put it together as a power point presentation about drugs that everyone here can use. The teachers were okay with my ideas. If I hadn't found this place I would probably be doing drugs and drinking heavily. I hardly drink at all now even though I'm at the legal age now. I've been independent since I was 15 and I've had to make my own decisions but since I've been here I look at things with a different understanding. (Extract of a portrait developed from an interview with Jenny 22/4/2010)

Jenny describes a quantum shift in her attitude towards education and self-image since joining *Stepping Out*. In some important ways, the locus of control over learning has shifted from the teacher to herself. 'When I was at school the teacher was in charge but now it's me', she states. From her perspective, 'being in control' means being able to study courses that are aligned more closely to her ambitions, having the opportunity to engage in creative writing and projects of interest, having the freedom to attend classes at times that suit her, and being able to participate in a hands-on approach to learning. The freedom, she describes, operates within boundaries. As she points out, there are rules such as courtesy, respect and manners, but she is treated like a human being rather than a 'brat child'. Jenny has struggled with drug dependency, fractured family relationships and lack of self-confidence but she now has a greater sense of agency and purpose in her life. One of the most persistent themes from research into these re-entry programs is their life-saving and life-enriching potential. Learning usually extends well beyond the acquisition of technical skills and competencies (though these are important) to the development of attitudes, values and dispositions that enable students to raise their self-worth, envision a more optimistic future and see themselves as young people with something of value to contribute to society.

Humanizing relationships: Connecting to others

The task of re-connecting alienated youth to education extends beyond a concern for individual identity to consideration of the ways in which young people function as members of a group. Education is above all a social process (Dewey, 2001), and whether students achieve that in school depends in no small measure on how well they relate to teachers, peers and others. Osterman (2000) asserts that students' need for belonging to a community is one of the most powerful factors in school engagement. In spite of the best intentions of many teachers, high schools are often considered to be large, impersonal and uncaring places. A high proportion of the students we interviewed had experienced harassment and bullying, often to the point where they were so emotionally damaged they could not continue their formal schooling. Many complained that they were devalued, belittled and treated disrespectfully by school authorities. Some spoke of fear, threat of retribution and punishment as the basis for learning rather than the development of relational trust and mutual respect between teachers and students. They regarded schools as coercive institutions that demanded high levels of compliance to petty rules and regulations. Those who did not fit the system often found themselves victims of 'technologies of exclusion' (Foucault, 1977) operating through sorting and streaming practices, discriminatory testing regimes, and punitive behavior management policies. Giroux (2006) suggests that the adoption of a zero tolerance approach to disciplinary issues has provided authorities with a quick and dirty way of kicking kids out of school. In an environment where the institutional norms are based on compliance and control 'it becomes easier to punish students rather than listen to them' (p. 161) and work to address their concerns.

Building relational trust (Bryk & Schneider, 2002)

Humanizing relationships (Noguera, 1995) seems an indispensable element in any attempt to connect young people to education. From what our young informants told us, teachers in re-engagement programs are usually more attentive to the relational aspects of learning than their counterparts in traditional high schools. Riley from *Stepping Out* recalls: 'I didn't connect with the teachers at school but here I can have a one-on-one talk with them. There's not the distance between teachers and students that there is at school and they treat you more as an adult.' His classmate, Cameron, expresses similar views. 'Our teachers become more of your mate than your enemy. They don't get grumpy and they give you a second chance'. Although teachers in these re-entry programs have instructional roles and responsibilities, students are more inclined to regard them as friends and/or mentors rather than overseers of their behavior and learning. Norms of reciprocity, integrity, mutual respect and shared responsibility come to the fore in the following remarks:

> We respect our teachers here. They don't just stand around telling us what to do. They are more your friend. They talk to us and we call them by their first name. If they tell us to do something we don't like we just do it. (Nancy: Youth Pathways)

> Our teacher, Julie, treats you for you. You give her respect and she gives it back to you. You can talk to her if you have a problem. She's more of a part time teacher and mostly friend. (Rosie: Merino Plains Applied Learning)

> The thing [about our community learning program] is that you're not singled out. It's not as strict as school but we do stick to the lesson times. If you are going to come in late you let [the teacher] know. It's about respect. You get what you give. (Toni: Merino Plains Applied Learning)

Building relational trust is the foundation for learning and, as Reggie's narrative illustrates, it begins by being treated 'like you are something'.

Reggie's story: 'The people here treat you like you are something'

> I've just turned 15 and I've been in foster care for about 6 years. When I first came into the Youth Pathways program I was 14 years old. I came because I wasn't allowed into high school. I had a history in primary school. When I had my older

sister there she used to get me out of trouble but when she left I got into trouble. My teachers called me a little shit and stuff like that. The principal even tried me to push me down the stairs. So I'd get on the roof and drop mud balls on the teachers. I was out of control. I got expelled just before I left grade 6 and went to a couple of other schools before joining Youth Pathways. Recently I got suspended from here and this is my second day back. I got on okay with my learning at primary school. I had a tutor called Susie who was a big help to me. In the morning I would have toast with her and if I wanted to have hot chocolate I would have to do some work. The people here treat you like you are something whereas the teachers at school treat you like you are nothing. I'm more of a hands-on person. I learn when I'm really calm. Sometimes I get angry and I won't do work. When I'm here there is one student that makes me calm. We get on really well. She's a bit like my sister and knows that when I walk out I am going to go off and have a smoke or just go up the hill. I'm not being removed I just remove myself so I don't flip out. It makes me feel good when I'm treated with respect. If high schools and primary schools were like this I would be in high school. Here I am in control of my action—no one else. Youth Pathways isn't just about writing down stuff. You do maths and writing but you also get to do hands on things. Yesterday I painted a T shirt—GTR with a car. We are doing maths right now. Some of the kids have made a couch and that involves measuring. They've also done up a lamp and an old TV. I enjoy all that sort of stuff. My carer has a mud brick house and I know how to render with water, cement and lime. My step brother does the rendering and I take the buckets up to him. When I finish here I might be going to TAFE to become a chef. Last night I cooked carbonara and tonight I'm doing spaghetti. How did I learn to cook? Someone showed me and I just learnt other things. I like to do my own thing, not simply follow the recipes. With the carbonara I looked at the ingredients on the tins and just throw it in and my friend said it was the best meal she had. I know a few chefs and hopefully I can get into the business. When I went to school in grade 5 I made restaurant business cards. I had a business going in the neighborhood house, before I started Youth Pathways, selling sausage rolls and home-made juice. I want to do this again and I can use the kitchen here. My older sister was pretty important to me but she lives in Queensland now. We were really close. Now that she is up there we don't really talk because it upsets me so much. (Portrait developed from a transcript of an interview with Reggie 21/4/2010)

Students need caring and trusting adults who can nurture relationships and create a stable learning environment. Although Reggie is far from settled in *Youth Pathways*—he is still searching for an anchor in his life—there are some signs of a turn-around in his attitude to schooling. He is involved in learning that is hands-on, useful and productive. He is treated with respect and feels he has an opportunity to make something of himself in the culinary world. Importantly, he is learning the art of self-control when it comes to managing his emotions.

Serving your time and starting afresh

Reggie has been given a second (perhaps last) chance to re-engage with schooling. This opportunity to start afresh in a non-judgmental setting is especially important to students re-entering schooling. 'Having a reputation', as they called it, meant that they were often targeted by teachers in mainstream schools because of past transgressions and misdemeanors. They contrasted this treatment with the reception they received in out-of-school learning centers. Speaking of the satellite learning program in Merino Plains, Bodie remarks 'When you come here you can start again', 'They take you as you are at *Stepping Out*. They don't judge me', says Bianca. Her classmate, Christine, gives a similar account of her experience.

Christine's story: 'Here no one judges you by what you've done'

I'm 14 years and 10 months old and I come from a foster home. I've been here about 4 weeks now. I went to Merino Plains High School but I wasn't getting on with the kids. I was getting behind and was easily distracted so I had a meeting with the teachers and they said that I should come to Stepping Out till I was a bit older and then I could go to TAFE. It's easier for mum to get me here because I only need to come three days. We have smaller classes than school and they focus more on your abilities. You get more attention and they concentrate more on you if you are having problems. Because everyone comes with problems we help each other out. That's why we get on so well. Here no one judges you by what you've done. I'm good at all my subjects except maths. I've had a lot of family problems so I got behind. I've just started private tutoring in Merino Plains. They're going to start me at year 7 maths and take me to year 9. I'm hoping to get into hairdressing. If I wasn't here I don't know what I would be doing. They told me to do home schooling but it's a bit isolating. I would probably study online. In two years time I hope to do my TAFE course in hairdressing and get an apprenticeship. I would like to stay in Merino Plains. It's big but not too big. (Excerpt from a transcript of an interview with Christine 9/6/2011)

Christine draws attention to several aspects of relational learning in *Stepping Out*. Small class sizes, which are far from the norm in conventional schools, enable her to receive individual support from her teachers when she encounters difficulties. Knowing that teachers focus on her abilities rather than her deficiencies is a comfort to her. There is a greater spirit of cooperation amongst students that partly arises from knowing that they have all come with the same problems. Not being judged for what they have done in the past is a far cry from their previous schooling experiences. Finally, flexible programs and school structures cater for students with out-of-school commitments.

Taking harassment seriously: 'They handle things differently here'

From our conversations with young people it seems that one of the defining differences between conventional high schools and re-entry sites is the way in which those in authority deal with bullying, racist harassment and violence against students. Teresa from *Beyond School* says she was teased a lot at school and when she lashed out she got into tons of trouble. 'Some people just didn't like me', she says. 'They pushed me over and made fun of me. The school really didn't take the matter seriously. When it continued to happen I just stayed in a common room'. Now enrolled in a Satellite applied learning course, Emily left school in year 9 after an altercation with a maths teacher but as she explains bullying was rife in the school. 'It started as name calling and led to people punching and stuff. People make up rumors and then they think that they are tough in front of their friends. I just dropped out of school and then fell pregnant.'

It would be unrealistic to suggest that the learning environment in re-entry programs is free of intimidation but there seem to be more effective approaches to dealing with potential conflicts. Marika from *Connexions* says they don't have much bullying in her group partly because 'all the kids here have come from the same background and they know how they feel and they don't want to do it here.' However, when it occurs teachers handle things differently. There's always four or five teachers in the class room and if a problem comes up they take you out of class and ask you what is happening.' This model of intervention, where problems are addressed in situ rather than being allowed to fester, is generally accompanied by an approach (Millei, 2010) where students and teachers seek to resolve disputes and conflicts through dialogue, counseling and negotiation rather than recourse to retribution. James explains how this operates in *Stepping Out*:

> When we had a little argument here earlier in the year the teachers just asked us what was wrong. They told us about the problem and then we just talked to them and we sorted it out. Rather than getting punished we were able to get the problem solved in this way.

Thomas from *Connexions* admits that he gets into trouble occasionally for 'speaking his mind' but says that his teachers are able to talk though problems with students. 'Not many kids clown around here', he says, 'but if they do, the teacher asks them to take a breather for a while. I like the way they trust you to just to go out a bit and it's your own choice if you come back.'

We do not want to overstate the success of these conflict resolution processes in re-entry programs. Students are sometimes suspended for serious infractions of behavior codes and a few have been asked to leave. However, there is a strong belief amongst young people that these are more welcoming and friendly places than schools. This was especially true for Indigenous students. Although Commonwealth and State laws in Australia impose responsibilities on schools and education systems to prevent and combat racism, many of the Indigenous students interviewed in this research study spoke of the destructive impact of racist behavior on their schooling. Simon from *Stepping Out* recalls a teacher 'that was really racist towards Aboriginal kids' and his classmate Louise commented: 'Because I was a Koori [Aboriginal] kid I used to get picked on. It was pretty pathetic really. Some kids there were a bit racist'. However, on the positive side she records: 'We had an aboriginal teacher in the school and she used to help me and take me out of class and work with me. That was good.' In the following portrait, Shirley, an Indigenous student contrasts her miserable time in school with that in the *Stepping Out* re-engagement program.

'I don't experience racism here'

> I went to my neighborhood primary school but I didn't get along with anyone. I got into fights and stuff. One day my friend and I came here but I didn't come much because I didn't know anyone here. At secondary school I was put into a spe-

cial education program but got kicked out because of fighting. This year I started off perfect coming every day and staying out of trouble. There were racist people at school but its different here. There are lots of nicer people and a couple of black kids. The maths is different because you can do it on the computer or on the paper. I like to do it on paper. I only come once a week but I would like to come every day. Outside of school I like AFL footy but I don't play much sport. I'm a Sydney supporter. When I'm not here I look after my nephews and nieces. I've got 5 of each and I do some cooking for them. If I were telling other kids about Stepping Out I would say that it is a great place where you get along with everyone and you don't get picked on or nothing like that. I don't experience racism here. People are just friends. (Extract from a transcript of an interview with Shirley 22/4/2010)

Consigned to an 'at-risk' and 'special needs' category at school, Shirley feels a stronger sense of connection to education in the *Stepping Out* learning center where relationships are based on trust, respect and regard for others. Importantly, she doesn't experience racism in this environment.

Developing support networks: Connecting to communities, resources and opportunities

A high proportion of the young people we interviewed have impediments to learning that cannot be solved by schools alone. The racism that young Indigenous students like Shirley encounter is not confined to schools—it penetrates many facets of social and economic life. Those students living independently (or coping with little family support) are very dependent on Centrelink [Welfare] allowances, and the provision of low rental housing accommodation, public transport, and health and social services. Little learning is possible for them without access to community resources, opportunities and networks to promote their financial, social and physical well-being. As we shall discuss in the next chapter, teachers in these sites spend a great deal of time and energy negotiating with government departments, community organizations and private businesses so that students can attend classes knowing that some of their most basic needs for accommodation, health and welfare have been met. Young parents enrolled in *Connexions* and *Stepping Out* are an especially vulnerable group in this regard. We have chosen to focus on their experiences to show both the extent of hardships and discrimination they face and the crucial role of social networks, community resources and mentoring arrangements in supporting their learning and aspirations for the future.

The stigma of young parenthood

According to the Australian Bureau of Statistics (2010) there are approximately 12,000 teenage pregnancies per year in Australia, but few schools have programs in place for pregnant or parenting teenagers to continue their education. As a consequence, the vast majority leave before completing secondary school certificates, thereby restricting their employment and further education prospects. They have enormous barriers to overcome in trying to sustain an education and cope with parenthood. Their situation is not helped by a tendency within the fields of research and public policy to define teenage pregnancy as a social problem (Yardley 2008; Pittaway, 2005) that leads to long-term financial burdens, social exclusion and diminished life chances for young parents and their offspring, and unreasonable economic burdens on society.

Informed by an 'at-risk view' of young parents, the neo-liberal state solution is to promote strategies that reduce teenage child-bearing rates and encourage young people to participate in the workforce and/or further education and training programs as part of an overall effort to improve economic productivity (Yardley, 2008). Young parents, especially single mothers, are generally accorded a low status in society. In Yardley's (2008) words, they 'are often perceived as a homogeneous group of immature, irresponsible, single, benefit-dependent, unfit parents who deviate from ideals of motherhood' (p. 671). Supposedly lacking in aspirations and moral fiber they are seen to be undeserving of community respect and empathy. However, as Yardley (2008) explains, a tendency to stereotype teenage mothers ignores the enormous differences that exist between individuals with regard to their aspirations, interests, lifestyles and family circumstances. Unfortunately, successful accounts of the ways in which young parents have built their identities around a set of life-affirming goals and achievements are swamped by negative and disparaging representations of their lives in the mainstream media.

Young mothers in our study gave graphic accounts of their experience of social stigma, both within school and their community. 'I started in year 9 at my local school but I got pregnant', says Rosemary. 'I didn't like school. Other kids would tell us to do stupid stuff and they got us into trouble. They said we were scum. We didn't have many friends and we wanted to keep to ourselves. I'm not sure how it affected my learning but I began skipping school and teachers weren't able to grade me last year.' Harassment and social isolation damaged Rosemary's school life to the point where she felt she had no choice but to leave. Jess spoke of the public humiliation and disapproving looks she encountered in her neighborhood. 'As a young mum you do get labeled', she says. 'There are some people who look at you funny like on the street but mostly you just walk away. One time I was having a smoke in my car and although my kids weren't in the car two old ladies came up and said that I wasn't allowed to do that.' 'There's a lot of stigma attached to being a young mum', says Rhiannon. 'It was horrible and very degrading at times. When you're walking down the street a lot of elderly people would look at you saying that you are too young to have a kid— it's the looks and it's the body language.' Caitlin experienced particularly savage forms of harassment and vilification, 'As a young mum you get spat on and you get dirty looks from some people', she stated. 'We're accused of using the tax-payers money to have our children but some people just don't realize the stories behind these young mums.' According to Yardley (2008), rather than being an avoidable mistake or accident, teenage motherhood often represents 'a normative, valued and respected life choice [for girls], whose mothers, aunts and grandmothers may indeed have been teenage mothers themselves' (p. 682).

Social networks

Given the extent of community prejudice and discrimination, it is not surprising that many young parents feel rejected and devalued by society. Lacking the self confidence and social networks to actively pursue vocational, recreational and education interests they are inclined to shut themselves off from society. It takes considerable courage to re-commit to education in these circumstances. Following a series of traumatic events in her life, twenty-three-year-old Hannah joined the young parents group of *Connexions*. Reflecting on her struggles and achievements she now sees herself as one of the successful graduates of a program which she credits for helping her to discover her 'real self'.

Hannah's story: 'I finally discovered my real self'

My story begins when I was 4-years-old. My parents divorced and mum left home to do her own thing. From 8 to 11 years of age I was sexually molested. When I hit high school I just wanted to rebel. I wasn't a naughty child but I was traumatized and I used to do silly things, like chew gum and talk in class. They would give me detention all the time but they didn't say 'go and see a counselor'. When I was 16 or 17 I dropped out of school. My grades went down because I just kept putting work aside. I put on a lot of weight and reached about 100 kg at one stage. Then I became bulimic and all of a sudden became really thin. It was my involvement with drugs and alcohol that led to me leaving school. Before joining Connexions I was with my ex-partner. He was very abusive both emotionally and physically—being a heroin addict—and I would get hit and stuff if I couldn't get money for him. My self-esteem got even worse and then I fell pregnant. I was homeless for about two years. Even when I was pregnant he used to hold knives against my throat. I had no one to turn to which made me worse. I had been with him for three years when I was referred to Connexions through the maternity health group. I finally broke up with him last year and have been with the program for one and a half years now. The Connexions program has been massive and the support from my teacher has been terrific. I was living in a unit with a bunch of alcoholics. Connexions helped me get a house. They gave me good references and helped with furniture. They also helped me get my license which was a big thing even though I didn't have a car. I do now. Just little things like this helped me with my confidence and encouraged me to learn so I can go back to uni—something that I'm passionate about. Without them I wouldn't be where I am today nowhere near it. At the end of 2008 I broke up with my ex-partner and moved in with my father. I got my car and now I'm living in my own two-story town house. It's looking pretty snazzy. I did Certificate 4 in Welfare Community Services and I was more confident. I finally discovered my real self. I can see myself in 10 years in marketing and public relations. I've always been a creative person. I draw now but at the moment I've been concentrating on my uni course, a diploma of professional writing and editing. In the first semester last year I started a Bachelor of Arts in psychology but found that it wasn't for me. I like writing speeches and presentations. A while ago I spoke to about 100 people and I also helped raise 2 grand for them. Before I joined the young parents group in Connexions I was trapped. It would have taken a dramatic experience to get me out of where I was. My health has improved since I've got off the drugs and I'm getting back into the learning mode. I am now able to express myself through my work. But there are so many young kids out there with just bad luck and they have no one to turn to. (Portrait developed from a transcript of an interview with Hannah, 12/3/2010)

In a myth-busting anthology of essays by young mothers, Davis (2004) claims that with enough support and the right opportunities young parents can overcome the isolation and social stigma of teen motherhood and become model students and highly successful individuals. There can be no better illustration of this possibility than Hannah's inspirational account of how she discovered her 'real self' from the depths of despair and depression. It is difficult to imagine a more emotionally and socially damaged life yet she managed to rebuild her identity around a set of life-affirming goals and educational aspirations. With an extraordinary level of support of her *Connexions* teacher, Hannah was able to acquire skills, resources and access to services that allowed her to imagine and embark on a more fulfilling, healthy and independent life.

Sen's (1999) notion of capabilities is helpful in understanding how education can promote the economic, social and political well-being in individuals and communities. *Connexions* played a key role in building Hannah's capabilities by assisting her to identify more clearly what she wanted to do with her life, by providing her with knowledge and skills to actively pursue education and employment opportunities, and by helping her to understand more clearly how her own economic and social circumstances might impede or support her choices. She now had a good reason for getting off drugs and getting back into a learning mode.

Learning in this context cannot be divorced from the social and economic realities of young parents' lives. A key feature of the young mothers' groups in the research sites is the social networking role they play in connecting students to health, welfare and counseling services, employment agencies and further education providers. Young parents are mentored by senior students and have a safe space where they can talk openly about their experiences of parenting, maternal health care and the day-to-day issues of survival. They speak with gratitude of teachers who go to extraordinary lengths to secure decent accommodation for them, assist them with child care and transport arrangements, and help them gain access to welfare services, work-experience placements, part-time employment, job agencies, TAFE courses and community programs.

Engaging pedagogies: Connecting to learning

Most students joining out-of-school learning centers do so because they have rejected or been rejected by mainstream schools. In many ways they have reached a point of 'no return' when it comes to re-engaging with conventional schooling. Although others may harbor the possibility of rejoining school to complete a secondary certificate or take advantage of broader curriculum offerings, this rarely happens. Why is this so? What is it about the alternative centers that students find appealing? According to our young informants, they are far more relaxed and enjoyable places than school. There are no bells to regulate daily activities. They don't have to wear school uniforms and in most programs they relate to teachers on a first name basis. Issues such as dress code, attendance, assessment deadlines and standards of behavior, which can be sources of contention in school, are dealt with in a more flexible and consultative fashion. 'Probably the most important thing here is the atmosphere' says Lucas. 'The satellite applied learning program has got a completely different feel to traditional school. It's more relaxed. It's not fearful. You get treated as an adult.' Rules and regulations about what students must study are less rigid. They are usually able to negotiate the number of subjects they wish to study to take account of part-time work and other commitments. These responses are not uncommon amongst students enrolled in out-of-school learning centers. Similar sentiments were expressed by the young people who participated in Mills and McGregor's (2010) Australian study of the success factors in re-engaging students in alternative schools.

'The way we learn is different to school'

A congenial learning environment is important but re-connecting disengaged learners to education also requires a rather different approach to teaching and learning than occurs in most mainstream classrooms. One way of describing the difference is around the notion of 'engaging pedagogies' (Zyngier, 2010)—those practices that sustain the interest, resolve and active involvement of young people in their learning. Our young informants were able to articulate, often in quite expressive language, what this meant. Brian remarks: 'The teachers in *Beyond School* make an effort to make programs suit the students. You get to do more hands on stuff and you can do your own things instead of what teachers tell you.' Gabriella from *Connexions* cuts to the quick with her remarks about curriculum relevance: 'You do learn some things at school that you don't need', she states, 'but here they cut out a lot of the bullshit and just teach you about things you need for life.' It's also about being accepted, respected and given the opportunity to do something worthwhile. Bullied, humiliated and rejected by her peers at school, seventeen-year-old Rosie enrolled in a *Satellite* program to gain work-place qualifications and improve her skills in literacy and numeracy. This is how she described the change in her experience of schooling.

Rosie's story: 'It's still school but you are learning'

I've been to many schools and I've been in and out of home. A few old friends of mine had been into the Satellite class and they said it's pretty good because you can do the work in your own time. I've been here since the beginning of the year. I come for 4 days a week for about 4–5 hours a day. On a typical day I grab a coffee, get my work set out and get stuck into it. We mostly do numeracy and literacy as well as personal studies. I completed years 7 and 8 I got half way through year 9 at school and now I am doing year 11 certificate courses. I've done RSA (Responsible Serving of Alcohol) and First Aid. That opens up some avenues of work. A first-aid certificate will not help you for a job but if you saw someone that needs help you could assist them. Our teacher treats you for you. You give her respect and she gives it back to you. You can talk to her if you have a problem. She's more of a part time teacher and mostly friend. She doesn't push you to do anything. She says it's in your own time—you learn this as you get into it. She gives you the work with instructions and if you need help you ask her and she gives you time to do it. Anne gets kids motivated. I've done a lot of things so far that could be useful for me. I spoke to Anne about a nursing course and she is going to follow that up for me. I've pretty much given up looking for new schools. So have a couple of my friends. They just hang out down the street. But I don't want to be like them. I don't associate with them that much but they say that it's pretty upper class in here and why would I hang out here. Yeah, they just can't see that I want to get a job and get a life. This place is better than ordinary school. It's still school but you are learning—you learn as you go really. You can take your work home or leave it. We had 6 weeks of doing acting and creative stuff that was really enjoyable. Our teacher has taught us to work in a team and she got me into a play. My health has improved since I joined this program. I get out of the house and talk to people and it does help. What would I say to the premier or the prime minister about the Satellite program? I'd tell them to go and teach here for a day. (Portrait developed from a transcript of an interview with Rosie 10/6/2010)

Rosie is under no illusions that she is still at school but makes an important distinction between 'school' and the space she now inhabits where you are actually learning. From her perspective, a more relaxed and flexible approach to learning coupled with a greater emphasis on individual support and tuition has opened her eyes to the benefits of education—something that she did not see at school. The smaller class seems to engender better relationships amongst students and teachers so that bullying is no longer an issue. Her teacher, Anne, sets the tone for a climate of acceptance and trust. 'You give her respect and she gives it back to you', says Rosie.

Learning different kinds of things in different ways

Many early school leavers share a common experience of bullying and an inability to cope with the regimented routines and regimes of control in the traditional high school. Ryan from *Beyond School* seems to fit this pattern, and he has a rather delightful way of expressing his feelings about the suffocating atmosphere of his classroom.

Ryan's story: 'I need air'

I'm 14 years old and I've been in Beyond School for 6 months. When I was in secondary school I got bullied a lot. They used to tease me about my hair. I let things build up and then I retaliated. I got suspended for three weeks but they put me on half days and I didn't get to do the practical stuff just the theory. When my best mate, Jim, was asked to leave the school I got to chatting to a teacher about things. Jim told me that he was going to Beyond School and I thought it would be good. So I finished up here. I just got distracted at school. We used to work for a straight 50 minutes and the windows and doors were shut and I need air. There were about 30 kids in my class. Here we get an opportunity to work on stuff. Everyone is treated equal and I find it better. We are learning different kind of things in different ways. The teachers here actually have a joke with you but they can get pretty tough at times. Yeah they give you a talking to at times and we've got boundaries. For the kids who smoke there is a smoking area and you have to smoke there. You're not allowed to eat lunch inside. There's to be no swearing and we've got to watch our language. You're not allowed to hit anybody. It's a safer place to learn here. My life has definitely improved since I've joined the program. If I weren't here I'd probably be kicked out trying to get into a new school. I've got more control over my life. In high school the teachers controlled you—'do this do that'—but here we get that sort of freedom. You still have to deliver things but not to the extent that I had to do there. You get more say about what you can do. We've been working on the car that you saw when you were last here. There a lot of learning involved in that. You had to use mathematics. When you see a bolt—about a 15 mm one—you say, 'Oh it fits'. With the mix thinners we had to learn about ratios. You've got to learn how to line things up, how much oil to measure out and how to calculate the size of the bolts that fit. We had to learn to work as a team. It's much better than sitting in a classroom. In woodwork we are building huge picnic tables and we're learning heaps of new things. At high school we would not be allowed to use the tools that we are allowed to use here—like the drop saw for instance. It's still a safety issue. We have to wear ear muffs and face masks but they give us a chance and people respect that. I'm year 8 this year. When I finish the course I'd like to be a mechanic. But I'm not one of those people who can sit down. Maybe TAFE is more hands on. (Extract of a portrait developed from a transcript of an interview with Ryan 20/4/2010)

Aside from a physical need for oxygen we can read Ryan's cry for air as a metaphor for his yearning for the space and freedom to pursue his own interests and aspirations beyond the perimeters of the school. Learning makes more sense now because theory is linked in a more direct and practical way to the things that interest him. Importantly, he is accorded a large measure of trust and responsibility that was denied to him at high school. Engaging pedagogies in Ryan's language amount to 'learning different kinds of stuff in different ways' –through working as a team, using his hands, applying knowledge in context, having a useful outcome, and seeing the connections between learning and life outside school.

Having fun: Learning that is personable and enjoyable

Ryan's narrative suggests that re-engagement with education is more likely to occur when students are able to make a personal connection with teachers and the learning environment. Having fun and not being bound by rigid structures is important to students like Bev:

> We don't just do maths and English and they make it fun so you want to learn. It's not just copying things off the board. I

like hands-on things. With normal school you know what you are going to do every day but in Connexions it is just random. You don't know what is going to happen. I like that. I don't like to have a timetable.

Similar sentiments emerge in the next portrait where Sonia contrasts her experience of social exclusion and failure at high school with that of a satellite course in Federation City which has lifted her spirits, given her a greater measure of ownership of her learning and a reason to come to school.

Sonia's story: 'You'd see the difference'

I actually enjoy coming here. It's heaps better than my previous school. The only subject I turned up for there was first aid because I wanted my certificate. I am enjoying my personal project about my dream job to own a bar and to be the bar attendant. I don't know what the main attraction is—alcohol maybe. I'm exploring how much it's going to cost, the types of people I'd want working in my bar, the location of the bar and so on. I'd try and get a loan from the bank to set it up and I'd do a hospitality traineeship. The costs and drawing up of the plan would involve maths as well. I'd get my dad to help with that. He's a plumber and he'd help me renovate the bar as well. Last night I wrote down a list of things I could do on my dream job and moving out of home. My previous project was on moving out of home. I won't move out until I get my Ps [probationary license so I have transport. I'm taking way less 'sickies' now and I'm getting on much better with my parents....I would like to get a hospitality traineeship next year and then get a job at a bar at the local pub. The applied learning course is a fun way of getting an education. The teachers are not like actual teachers. They are the best teachers that I've ever had and I've learnt a lot from them. There's no bells here which is good. At school you get your subjects and to do projects but here you get to choose your projects. You get your outcomes from the program and you get your applied learning certificate. I smile almost nonstop in this course and it's fun. I get to have a laugh whereas at school you get told to sit down and do this and do that. You don't hear many raised voices in class. Trust me; if you went to school and had to learn and then you came here you'd see the difference. (Extract from a portrait developed from a transcript of an interview with Sonia 9/3/2010)

When young people cannot or do not form a relationship with adults or peers at school there is every likelihood that they will disengage or drop out of school (Smyth et al., 2000). The teachers in Sonia's satellite applied learning program are not like 'actual teachers'—rather they relate to students in a personable way that promotes a greater sense of fun, and freedom. Being able to choose a course of study and having a tangible outcome, in the form of a training certificate, makes for more meaningful education.

'We get to have a say'

If there is a common thread running through young people's narratives it is the notion of power over learning or the lack thereof when it comes to mainstream schools. Students feel a stronger connection to education when they have a meaningful say in what they learn, how they learn and how that learning is to be assessed. 'In school you don't get a choice of what you learn' says Amy, 'but in *Stepping Out* we choose what we learn and we enjoy it because it's not forced on us.' Hayley who participates in a satellite applied learning program says she has the freedom to do things herself. 'Instead of teachers giving you projects they let you pick your own project' she says, and adds, 'we don't get treated like kids here unless we are acting like kids.'

Connexions students get to have a say about the norms of acceptable conduct in the center, as Vanessa explains:

> We came up with the rule that says you will be asked to leave for a day if you smoke outside the building. It's to help people give up smoking or for some people who can't have smoke around them. We also agreed that there should be no mobile phone calls in class because students were having conversations and not doing their work. It just disturbs the other students.

Establishing norms of behavior through dialogue and negotiation with students rather than foisting them on them helps to create a stronger sense of communal ownership of the learning environment and reduce the likelihood of friction between teachers and students. As opposed to the authoritarian culture of high schools where conflicts and behavioral matters are often dealt with in punitive ways, there seems to be a greater inclination for teachers and students in re-engagement programs to talk through problems. In the following portrait, Jordan explains what 'having a say means' in the satellite applied learning program in Federation City.

Jordan's story: It's a process of negotiation

On Wednesday everyone sits down for a cooked lunch and we talk over problems we might have. If you are angry with people you just bring it out in the open—like 'I'm angry at you because you threw a pen at me'. If it's a massive problem—like someone smells really bad—we refer to them as an unnamed person rather than using their actual name. There doesn't seem to be any problems because most people come from the same backgrounds. I have never seen anything like it....Regarding the camp, some people who have had behavior issues need to make a case as to why they should go. It's a process of negotiation. If 100 % of the group says 'yes we want this guy to go' but the teachers said 'no we don't' we could still decide that this guy should go because the teachers still only have one vote. The exception might be if someone punched a person in the face then the teachers would make the decision. (Extract from a portrait developed from a transcript of an interview with Jordan, 19/4/2010)

Democratic decision making of this kind was not apparent in all out-of-school re-engagement programs, but students generally do have a more active role in negotiating policies and practices that impact on their learning and daily routines. The notion of power sharing described by Jordan is a radical departure from what happens in most high schools where student voices are often silenced or suppressed.

Re-connecting young people to education is a challenging and difficult task, especially when many have lost faith in schooling and/or lack the economic and social resources to support their learning. However, our young informants have given us reasons to be cautiously optimistic about what can be achieved in out-of-school learning centers.

Have these re-engagement programs made a difference?

If I hadn't found Connexions I would be like a hermit really just waiting for my Centrelink money. I would go shopping then come home and do nothing again. Since joining this group I have learnt to be open and not to be shy. You can do things you want to do but you have to jump up and speak up. Once you couldn't say boo to me but I'm more confident and outgoing. It's made me more a person than what I was. I am getting to be the person that I want to be.' (Amanda: Connexions Young Parents Group)

According to the advocates of high-stakes testing, success in schooling is largely a measure of student proficiency in literacy and numeracy. If that is all that matters then re-engagement programs that cater for some of the most disadvantaged students may struggle to make their mark. This is not to say that academic achievement should not be regarded as an important goal of education, but it has to be placed in the context of young people's lives and circumstances. The growth in confidence and self-assurance that Amanda has gained from her involvement in the young parents' group has helped her to become a more independent and outgoing person. Social learning of this kind cannot be calibrated by standardized test scores, yet it is surely a foundation for meaningful engagement with learning.

From the many conversations we have had with young people it is abundantly clear that alternative learning centers have raised their expectations of education and created opportunities that did not exist in mainstream schools. For some students, this has taken on life-saving proportions. Mitchell confided 'If I hadn't come to *Connexions* I would either be dead or in the gutter. That's how bad it was in my previous school'. Jessie, a young woman with serious medical issues, said her life before coming into *Connexions* was 'just crap'. 'Before I was here I was heading towards 'juvie' (juvenile detention)', she says. 'Now my health is improving a bit now and no one picks on me.' While some students still struggle to reconnect with education on a regular basis, many say they come with a spring in their step because it's their choice to do so. Contrary to popular beliefs, many have aspirations to further their education, gain worthwhile employment, make a contribution to society and/or become better parents. They often tell us that they are less aggressive now and interact in a more friendly and cooperative manner with their peers and teachers. Many report improvements in their health, well-being, self-esteem and confidence. Moreover, they can see a more optimistic future for themselves and have greater faith in the possibilities of education. Without this kind of re-connection life would be bleak they say. Sophie's account of her experience captures some of the life-changing nature of these programs.

Sophie's Story: 'This has been life saving and life changing for me'

My name's Sophie. I'm 21-years of age and I had my baby, Billy, when I was 17. I found out I was pregnant in year 10. I had about 5 months in year 11 at the Federation City High secondary campus but left in May and my baby was born in August. I tried to enroll in school again but there was a lot of pressure on me. Then the hairdresser next door passed my name on to the coordinator of Connexions in late 2006. He was starting a young parents' group—basically to help young mum's out there—and there were only four of us at the time. We did art and craft and jewellery making. On one occasion we had our hair done and we went out to tea with the mayor in a limo. Katrina, the hairdresser, did all our hair and then we went to Myer [Department Store] and got our makeup done. Frank, our teacher, was trying to make us feel good about ourselves. At the time my self-esteem wasn't very good because there were nasty rumors about young mums. It was difficult living in this town, so much so that I didn't have my son for the first twelve months. I joined the circus in an interstate city for a while and then Frank helped me get my son back after a year. He got me enrolled in Certificate 2 Hospitality Front of House and then I did my little thing and took off. But he never gave up on me. Then I started going back to young mums. I didn't feel like getting in full-time study to start with. This year I applied for a traineeship in nursing. I didn't get into that but at the minute I am doing a pre course for nursing which will give me maths and English. Frank got me into that as well as the interviews. He never gave up even when I was in the circus. I have spoken to young mums and there are no programs like this anywhere. They can only dream about them. The only consistency in my life has been Frank. He wants what is best for the mums and has helped me a lot with counseling when I was getting stressed out. He has asked me to be a role model for the younger ones in the group. I can't believe that he never gave up on me. He dug his heels in and he made me believe that I was better than I think I was. If I hadn't of found my way in here I'd be drugged and I wouldn't have my son. This has been life saving and life changing for me. But it's not just me he helps. Another thing is that when he tries to get you into schooling it's not broad—it's made to suit you. When my brother got kicked out of school he didn't have a place like this to go to. It wasn't thought of. All places should have programs like this. It shouldn't be just young mums. It's where my son can get a check up and where I can go to school. (Portrait developed from a transcript of an interview with Sophie 8/6/2010)

Are the programs sufficiently demanding and challenging for students? Where do they lead to in terms of further education options? There is a perception in some quarters that these off-school learning centers are for 'drop-outs'—students who have been rejected by school. 'They think that it's for kids who are hooked into drugs and stuff or retarded' says Laura, 'But', she adds defiantly 'I just say, you don't know nothing about *Stepping Out* so shut up.' Not all students are satisfied with what's on offer in these programs. Jamie is involved in a satellite applied learning program that appears to him to be under-resourced and lacking in rigor, especially when it comes to preparing him for a senior school certificate.

> I reckon that it would be better if we had more funding. I reckon that there could be more work in our program. The breaks are too big especially at our outdoor center. I liked to keep occupied there. It's a bit laid back. That's not really my thing. Yeah I pretty much I like a structured kind of environment. If someone gave me an opportunity to go back to mainstream school I might take it but I would be behind. I'm trying to finish year 12.

What of the longer term employment and post-school education prospects for these young people? Anecdotally, we know of students in re-engagement programs who have completed TAFE courses, undertaken university studies, gained apprenticeships and found meaningful employment. These individuals have become models and, in some instances, mentors for students. However, these success stories need to be placed alongside the grim statistics of youth unemployment and structural inequalities in regional communities. The vast majority of students who re-engage with education in alternative learning centers lack not only the cultural and social capital of their middle class peers but are further disadvantaged by the discontinuous and disruptive nature of their schooling. Students in these circumstances need access to better educational services, qualified teaching staff and courses that will open up academic as well as vocationally oriented pathways. On the question of equity, Teese and Polesel (2003) claim that under current funding arrangements:

> public investment in making the curriculum more socially inclusive relies almost wholly on the willingness and ability of teachers acting in isolation, and often under adverse conditions, to compensate for weaknesses in student cultural capital, on the one side, and in curriculum design, on the other. (p. 197)

The willingness of teachers to go the extra yards for students has been a recurring theme in the portraits presented in this chapter. It does, however, raise the question of the sustainability of these programs. What will happen when these committed educators move on?

Concluding remarks

Young people have the capacity to speak on matters of education, but they are rarely accorded the authority to do so. In this chapter we have tried to give voice to their concerns, aspirations and hopes for the future. In selecting portraits that illustrate their lives and experiences it has not always been easy to strike a balance between accounts of sadness and joy, despair and hope, and opportunities and constraints. We have not glossed over the emotional scars of schooling nor the unjust practices inflicted on young people but we hope their narratives convey something of their courageous spirit, resilience and capacity for re-inventing their lives around more optimistic goals. Echoing Lawrence-Lightfoot's (2009) words expressed in the introduction to Olson's (2009), *Wounded by School,* the students in our study 'become both the narrators and protagonists of their tales, and in so doing experienced an emerging sense of agency' (p. xiv). In identifying and documenting what Lawrence-Lightfoot calls the 'litany of lacerations' (p. xiv) of school they offered insights into what might be done to make educational institutions more just and compassionate places for young people. Students also had much to say about the support and care they received from teachers and 'significant others' in re-engagement programs—a theme we pursue in the next chapter.

CHAPTER 5

Hearing the Story Again—This Time from Adults

Introduction

To this point our account has focused chiefly on young people's narratives of education. This has been a deliberate decision on our part because we believe they are silent witnesses to what happens in schools and their voices are often unheard in the corridors of policy makers. In the previous chapter they gave us graphic and compelling descriptions of the toxic effects of inequality on their lives (Smyth, Down & McInerney, 2008), the depressing and irrelevant nature of much of the learning in high schools, and the stigma arising from a deeply ingrained sense of failure that characterized their school days. However, they also revealed that they were not merely hapless victims of injustices but were active agents in speaking back from the margins (Smyth, 2010; te Riele, 2011). Importantly, they had some perceptive things to say about the conditions in the out-of-school learning centers that enabled them to turn around their attitudes to education and life more generally. These sites also brought them into contact with adults who cared about them as people, encouraged them to think positively about their futures, and enabled them to access and mobilize material and cultural resources to support their identity formation (Wyn, 2007).

In this chapter we want to re-tell the story of re-engagement with schooling from the point of view of the teachers, program managers, school support staff and 'significant others' who, in various ways, contributed to the education and development of the young people in our study. It is appropriate that we consider a spectrum of adult perspectives because schooling is a complex endeavor that relies heavily on inter-sectoral collaboration between educators, health, welfare and youth support agencies, and community organizations. How do adults in these fields describe the issues confronting young people in adverse circumstances? How do they support them to become more independent, resourceful and optimistic individuals? What are the impediments to their work? In keeping with the representational strategies used throughout the text, we will explore these questions through portraits and extended quotes from adults interviewed in the research sites.

Teachers' stories

> The teachers in Stepping Out are super tolerant. Students lose the plot from time-to-time and they don't have the ability to sit still and just do the work. One girl talked about dealing with drugs to get money. She reported her dad three times. She's 16 and deals with that stuff. Academically they are not year 11 or 12 standard and kids coming over at year 10 level. There's been things happening in the family and they haven't been attending on a regular basis. There is a big drug culture in the town and binge drinking is commonplace. The girls are placed at risk because the guys they hang out with are a lot older and many of them are predatory. Most of them enjoyed primary school and as soon as they hit secondary school and they stopped playing sport...They need someone who listens to them. (Julie, Satellite Applied Learning Teacher, 25/5/2011)

During the course of our research we were fortunate to meet dedicated teachers like Julie who were prepared to persevere with students in the most difficult circumstances. In the main, the teachers we met were understanding and tolerant people with a broad range of knowledge and skills that they brought to bear in developing curriculum around the interests and needs of young people. In many respects the backgrounds of the seven teachers we interviewed were not dissimilar to their colleagues in mainstream schools. The flexible-learning centers in which they taught were administered, staffed and resourced through a public education system. All were nominally attached to a local high school. Although most had elected to teach in an alternative school setting, they did not necessarily bring with them finely tuned pedagogies for engaging disaffected students. Typically these were developed in conjunction with colleagues and students in a learning environment that gave them the space and opportunity to innovate and foster the relational aspects of learning largely missing in more conventional schools. Teachers like Julie had much to tell us about the challenging aspects of their work, the issues confronting young people, the conditions that seem to promote student engagement and the factors that sustain their passion for teaching. We have collated their stories around four intersecting themes:

- Visions of success
- Connecting to young lives
- Unauthorized methods
- Making a commitment to the humanity of students.

Visions of success

Writing about the difficulties of educating poor and culturally diverse children in the United States, Delpit (1995) claims that 'prospective teachers are exposed to descriptions of failure rather than models of success' (p. 177) in teacher education programs and schools. The widespread use of labels, such as 'at-risk, 'disadvantaged', 'underclass' and 'learning disabled' to categorize young people helps to normalize a discourse of failure around social class and ethnicity. Many teachers tend to take for granted that children from low-socioeconomic and culturally different backgrounds cannot be expected to achieve as well as white middle-class students. 'We teach teachers rationales for failure, not visions of success', argues Delpit (1995, p. 178). From our conversations it was evident that the teachers in the re-engagement programs were sustained by a belief that students in their care could succeed in schooling and make something worthwhile of their lives. Invariably, they talked up the accomplishments of young people in re-engagement programs who, against the odds, completed secondary school and TAFE certificates, went on to university, secured apprenticeships, found meaningful employment, and gained recognition for their artistic achievement, enterprise and service to the community. Success could also mean getting along better with others, gaining parenting skills, overcoming anger issues, or just feeling better about oneself. Notwithstanding the impediments, these teachers held 'visions of success' for young people. Lauren who teaches in *Connexions* spoke of the significance of personal relations and engendering a spirit of optimism and hope amongst students:

> The basic thing that I see is that the kids need to have one person who believes in them. They just need to know that somebody thinks that they can do just that little bit better. They need to know that they are doing okay for all the things that are happening in their lives that one person who believes in them knows that they could have something better. They need to know there is hope and to have a belief that life will get better. Whether it's fortunate or unfortunate, I have to trust that as a team that what we say is affirming to the student that we are dealing with and I'm going to play a small part of that journey. (Lauren, Connexions Work, 11/6/10)

Beutel (2010) suggests that the protracted contact that teachers have with young people places them in an ideal position 'to act as role models and "significant others" in their lives and to especially help those who find life's circumstances stressful and a threat to their well-being' (p.78). The pedagogic relationships Lauren and her colleagues have with marginalized students goes beyond instruction and information giving to mentoring arrangements that support 'the ongoing academic and social development of students, both inside and beyond the classroom' (Beutel, 2010, p. 85). This is demanding work and teachers occasionally have to detach themselves a little from the intense emotional labor that goes with the job. As manager of *Stepping Out*, Kate is responsible for curriculum planning, preparation of individual learning plans, student counseling, parent engagement, staffing matters and the day-to-day running of the center. She has to deal with distressing situations in her work, but like Lauren she is sustained by a sense of hope and the possibility of making a difference for her students. She does not allow herself to dwell too much on the past but looks to the future for positive changes—even if it means looking some distance ahead.

'We never talk in any other terms except the future'

> I've always had a passion for disengaged kids. When this job at Stepping Out was advertised I took the step and went into the unknown. I've never looked back. There was no handbook for the program. To some extent, it based on Connexions in Federation City so that's the model we followed. Originally it was set up in a youth center but because it was used by the whole community it wasn't a suitable venue. So we moved here and it's worked out wonderfully well. I've a background in education research which has helped me. I'm very strong on making the community responsible for these kids and getting them to

say, 'we'll take care of them'. I never pass up an opportunity to go and talk to community groups about them. When I get a bad kid from the capital city I hope that the good kids here will have an effect on them. We never talk in any other terms except the future.

How do I sustain my energy and passion for my working with these kids? I've got a beautiful supportive husband and my love of race horses keeps me going. I have other interests as well. In this place you are always helping kids so you don't feel down. I know I sound cold but you can't allow yourself to think too much about the upsetting things. To some extent I live in fantasyland. We might not have an effect on this child but I might have an effect on that child. As a staff we unload on each other and there's always plenty of laughter. We have a great staff and work as a real little team. It's a privilege to work with these kids and to make a difference to their lives. (Extract from a portrait developed from a transcript of an interview with Kate, 9/6/2010)

Kate is quick to acknowledge that not all students are lovable, but she believes that even the so-called bad kids from the city can succeed with the support and encouragement of teachers and peers. She identifies several facets of re-connecting young people to schooling: first, the need to engender a spirit of hope in young people by looking optimistically to the future rather than dwelling on a dark past and giving students an opportunity to start afresh with their learning; second, bringing the community on board so that responsibility for transforming young lives becomes a communal task and not something confined to schools; and, third, a willingness on the part of teachers to adapt curriculum to suit the needs of young people and to work in unconventional ways.

Unauthorized methods

A recurring theme in teachers' accounts of working with alienated youth is the importance of developing pedagogies that are grounded in a knowledge of students' lives and experiences rather than slavishly following what Kincheloe and Steinberg (1998) label 'authorized methods' or officially sanctioned approaches to teaching and learning. Darling-Hammond (1997, argues that American schools (and we would suggest Australian high schools, too) are deeply rooted in a bureaucratic tradition that goes back to a factory model of the 19th century. Despite some changes, 'most are still organized to impart a largely fact-based, rote-oriented curriculum through structures that do not allow long-term teacher-student relationships or in-depth study' (p. 47). Constrained by a hierarchical decision-making system '[t]eachers follow the rules and procedures...and students are processed according to them. (p. 47). In spite of calls by middle school advocates for a more integrated and dialogic approach to education, a didactic or transmission model of teaching prevails in many secondary schools.

As the mania for standardized testing has taken hold, narrow and instrumental indicators of what constitutes good teaching and learning have come to exercise a powerful (if not totalizing) influence on teachers' work. Curriculum control is reinforced by the widespread (and uncritical) adoption of 'teacher-proof packages' such as Madeline Hunter's teacher/supervision model which has found its way into thousands of education programs and school districts in the United States. The belief that teachers can enter a classroom with a pre-ordained view of what works with any group of students under any set of conditions does not stack up in practice—something confirmed by the teachers we spoke to in out-of-school learning centers. Felicity, who teaches in the *Connexions* program at Federation City, has her own take on what is needed to turn young lives around. 'It's all about finding the hooks', she says—those points of engagement with significant individuals and groups who can connect them to learning, employment and social opportunities.

'It's all about finding the hooks'

It's a journey with these young ones. I have to case manage and teach 16 kids in Connexions. It's a pastoral role but I have to be proactive in talking to different agencies, like housing and so on, and working with psychologists, parents, nannas and whoever. You have to be a bit of a detective to find the significant others in their lives. Our welfare role can't really be separated from teaching responsibilities. Working out their barriers to education and linking into their learning plan is what we do. From my experience every student goes off the rails at some point. They might be traveling along nicely and then something happens. I'm a strong believer that we couldn't have success here at Connexions if we didn't have a strong team of teachers, youth workers and counselors. We see some fantastic changes in the kids but it's not just because of me. It's the result of the team. The most effective professional development you have is the teachers working together. You are your own greatest resource.

There are plenty of obstacles to success for our students. Discipline is a big issue for kids in a mainstream school. Often

Hearing the Story Again—This Time from Adults

they get angry with the teachers and end up in the principal's office. Dysfunction in the classroom leads to anger and outbursts. Anxiety issues linked with depression and lack of confidence are a problem, especially with young girls. Some of them are bullied on the bus or whatever and they reach a state where they're not able leave their house. There are boys who need more hands-on learning and more one-to-one work in class. They have missed out on those building blocks in primary school. When they get to high school they need one to one but you can't get that in a class of 25 kids so they can't learn and they can't engage. I reckon 4 students are about the maximum we can work with. As well, there are drug and alcohol issues. Many are infatuated with the bong and they draw it everywhere. There are housing barriers so you need to work with providers like Uniting Care which is the main one in Federation City. Some of the kids are homeless and they're used to sleeping on couches.

The way to handle the problems is to develop a relationship with these kids—that is the key thing. I don't know how we managed without mobile phones, texting, making meetings. One kid I phoned didn't even know where he was. I had to Google the street and I had go and get him. He came in and we had a great session. You want them to phone you and tell you that they can't make it to a meeting, just looking for those points of engagement. Even when you are doing a word activity, you don't know which word will spark something. It's all about finding the hooks. If you looked at the history of their case notes you would see all the records of the people I ring and the people I had contact with—I keep good notes and lesson plans. What worked last week might not work this week. I'm constantly saying 'what am I going to do to make maths more interesting today'? You try lots of different things. We are tracking a couple of kids this year to find out what is working with them. One of our students, Natasha, was anxious and depressed when she started here 4 years ago. But she finished her year 12 and got into do education at university. She has deferred to come here and volunteer. She's still got issues but wow she is now going to be a teacher. That was a lovely story and we have had some students go on to university. I think the students are seeing different adult role models here and they get positive reinforcement and encouragement here. There was so much work put into Natasha by so many people—particularly from the art people who gave her so much confidence. The whole person needs to be looked at. You never know if what you are doing is going to have an impact. If you show the kids that you will persist with them then they get the message that we care about them. You build up a good-will bank and then you can come in with the hard discipline stuff. You can't do that when you start off. I did something wrong with a boy I had worked with for years. I undermined his trust just like that. Sometimes you walk on egg shells.

One student is an amazing photographer and I've put her into touch with someone in the City Council. Any young person needs to be connected to the community. If you are good at sport you need to be in a club. I had one young mum come to the local choir. They need to meet other people in the community. I'm getting kids into music through drumming. It's a very effective program to engage young people. It's a one-hour-week program for 10 weeks and we'll do that across campuses. We are looking at metaphors like rhythms of life. You can't make a wrong note on a drum. You have to be savvy about the things you need to take on board. (Extract of a portrait developed from a transcript of an interview with Felicity, 6/4/2011)

Reading Felicity's account of the joys, complexities and dilemmas of teaching in a re-engagement program, one is struck by the absurdity of the ideas promoted by advocates of school/teacher effectiveness. Professional expertise, as Kincheloe and Steinberg (1998) explain, is 'an uncertain enterprise as it confronts constantly changing, unique and unstable conditions' (p. 10). It cannot be codified or reduced to a set of technical strategies that can be applied in any school context. As Felicity points out, the idiosyncratic nature of teaching means that what works with a particular individual one day may not work the next. Although curriculum frameworks are a point of reference, individual learning plans and education pathways have to be negotiated with students on a case-by-case basis. Teaching and welfare roles are inseparably linked in situations which call for a high level of co-operation amongst educators, health professionals, youth workers, counselors and welfare agencies. From Felicity's perspective, re-engagement with learning means building relational trust, giving positive reinforcement and showing young people that you are prepared to hang in with them when the going gets tough—even if it feels like you're walking on eggshells at times. Felicity's story reinforces the view that teaching is a complex activity that cannot be easily categorized as a scientific or technical process. According to Rose (2006) it operates as much by feel as reason. Teaching well means:

> ...knowing one's students well and being able to read them quickly and, in turn, making decisions to slow down or speed up, to stay to a point or to return later, to underscore certain connections, to use or forgo a particular illustration. (p. 418)

Felicity knows a good deal about the life history of her students and their families. She feels a sense of connection to the community and is prepared to stand up for young people when she sees that they are unjustly treated.

Connecting to young lives

Young people have multidimensional lives and schooling or education is but a fragment of their identity. This is sometimes lost on educators. One of the most consistent criticisms students level at traditional high schools is the lack of connection between what they learn in class and their own lives and experiences. Palmer (2007) suggests that good teachers possess a capacity for connectedness insofar as '[t]hey are able to weave a complex web of connections among themselves, their subjects, and their students so that students can learn to weave a world for themselves'. (p. 11)

From our observations, connecting learning to student lives (Smyth, Down & McInerney, 2008; Prosser, Lucas & Reid, 2010) is a major priority for teachers in re-engagement programs. As coordinator of *Beyond School*, Stephen is responsible for developing an education program for students who have opted out of (or been forced to leave) mainstream schooling. Ranging in age from 13 to 15 years, many have reached a point of crisis in their lives. Stephen believes that gains in academic achievement for these students can only be realized with an enormous investment in the time, resources and personnel to connect the social and emotional aspects of students' lives to learning. This requires small class sizes, a hands-on approach to learning and individual learning plans in which curriculum is developed around the student's histories and experiences rather than fitting the student into the curriculum. Teaching in this environment demands patience, understanding and consistency when it comes to expectations and norms of students' behavior. Above all, it requires a high degree of collaboration and cooperation amongst teaching colleagues.

Developing a curriculum around the child

> In Stepping Out we look at the history of the individual and try to develop a curriculum around the child rather than develop the child around the curriculum. In most of the cases what has been offered is totally secondary to their economic and social

needs. In many instances they are quite competent but they have lost the capacity to do the work because they just think they can't do it. I reckon that 80% of the cause of their disengagement is to do with social and emotional factors and as little as 15–20% relates to the formal academic aspects of learning. We have some kids who didn't access school last year. They need to be connected with the social and emotional side of their lives before they can achieve academically. Some kids are very sharp with fractions and can measure ratio in paint in a practical sense instead of linking it back into page 49 of a year nine maths book.

Our kids have an Individual Learning Plan (ILP). It becomes the basis of reporting to parents and is central to all that we do. When we develop the ILP we try to be a bit flexible in doing what the child wants to do. We do it in a team situation with the kids and it's critical that everyone follows the ILP to the letter. We broker the plan with every kid but it does have some underlying fundamentals that relate to norms and expectations of behavior. The ILP is a living document that gets tossed at them every day. Their plan is in front of them every day and it gives them a guide to what they have to achieve.

I feel a bit inadequate at times but as a team we debrief for an hour or more every night. As four or five heads we usually come up with common ground. We often get more from listening to the kids. The other good thing is that older kids support the new kids. It's a mentoring arrangement that works okay. In a workforce like ours it's really important to collaborate and support each other. It's a team agreement and we are consistent in handling the kids' behaviors.

Beyond School has improved the kids' sense of worth and connection to school. The kids are starting to build a social fabric among themselves but we find it hard to maintain when we get over 6–7 kids in the class. Things can go awry very quickly. Most of these kids have one or two people who push the wrong buttons and then they arc up. They don't understand these kids. Some days kids can come in and work and then it goes to hell. We have street fights that come into school. There are signs of improvement in our relations with their parents. I make contact with the parents once a week and I think that is critical. In a lot of cases the parents agree with anything and sometimes there is inappropriate parenting. The consistency we show here has to have a connection to home and most of these parents are very supportive of what we do. I think the kids' life chances and their opportunities are being increased exponentially because there is a part of their life where they have stability. When they see where they are going they can connect that with what they need to do. (Extract of a portrait developed from a transcript of an interview with Stephen conducted on 11/6/2010)

Although Stephen has little to say about the specific content of the curriculum and pedagogies to engage students, he makes the point that teachers must first connect to the emotional and social lives of young people. Mastery of the academic learning is highly contingent on building students' self confidence, creating opportunities for social learning, and developing supportive networks for young people, such as peer-mentoring programs. In this context, the Individual Learning Plan becomes a useful (but flexible) tool for developing education goals and pathways around the specific interests, aspirations and needs of students. Stephen is under no illusions about the difficulties of re-engaging young people with learning, but he believes that caring individuals and a humane learning environment can make a big difference when it comes to improving their education and life chances.

Making a commitment to the humanity of students (Ayers, 2004)

The caring adults most trusted and respected by young people made it clear that they saw the potential, not the pathology in young people. One of the most moving encounters we experienced in our research took place before an interview with Robbie, a young student enrolled in the *Beyond School* program. In something of an unexpected move, Robbie was introduced to us by his teacher, Barry. Visibly angered by the way he had been rejected by his previous school, Barry hailed the boy as a success story with the potential to succeed at tertiary education level. In an emotionally charged voice he exclaimed, 'He could be a lawyer'. Barry revealed in a most dramatic way the notion of teachers as advocates for students by speaking out against unjust school practices and making a commitment to the humanity of students (Ayers, 2004).

Writing about the moral commitment of teaching, Ayers (2004) asserts that all students bring two powerful, propulsive, and expansive questions with them into every classroom. Though largely unstated—perhaps even unconscious—they are nonetheless essential. 'Who in the world am I, or who am I in the world?'

What in the world are my choices and chances? (p. 32) Teachers cannot answer these questions, for they lie in the hearts and minds of students themselves. One of the tasks of teachers is to convince students:

> often against a background of "obedience training school" that there is no such thing as receiving an education as a passive receptor or inert vessel…All real education is and always must be self-education. (p. 33)

The second task, says Ayers, is to demonstrate, as Barry did, that they are on the side of the student. This does not mean uncritically accepting whatever they do or say or abandoning codes of conduct. However, it does mean taking a stand against unfair and discriminatory structures and policies, creating spaces where students can speak back to the perpetrators of injustices, actively rejecting deficit discourses about students and their families, and seeking common ground to build growth and development.

In the previous chapter we recounted student experiences of schooling in an environment where conflicts were generally resolved through counseling and conciliation rather than recourse to punitive behavior measures. Teachers in these out-of-school centers were more inclined to create 'islands of decency' (Ayers, 2004, p. 34) where the most fraught issues about young peoples' lives could be talked about respectfully, candidly and deeply. They were also inclined to take greater risks in securing support for students. Frank, who teaches a program for young parents, offered the following insight into the humanitarian nature of his work.

This is life-saving work

> Once the young parents trust you they don't need our help but if we let them go away they would stay on welfare for the rest of their life and the cost is huge. This is a much better option. Some days we might have six paying customers and 6 non-paying customers [i.e. people who don't turn up]. This is life-saving work. We have girls that could well commit suicide if they knew they couldn't be there. One girl was in yesterday and she was in a bad state. It may seem that we are pushing the boundaries but we are not operating under the umbrella of the school. The school leaders know what we are doing by bending the rules: they turn a blind eye. If I need a washing machine [for a girl] I just go and buy one. What we do here is incredibly important. The proof will be in thirty years' time when I won't be around. (Excerpt from a portrait developed from an interview with Frank, 6/5/2011)

In many ways, these teachers are engaged in life-saving work but according to Andrew, an education administrator, they are constrained by funding arrangements and institutional politics that subvert the interests of students to that of the bureaucracy and management. 'It should always have been about how the organization can benefit the student not how the student can benefit the organization', says Andrew.

Teachers, parent volunteers, integration aides and school administrators carry out their work in conjunction with 'significant others' in schools and communities. What do these people have to say about the conditions that enhance young people's re-engagement with education? What particular insights can they bring to the questions of educational disadvantage and inequality?

'Significant others' stories

Although some school reformers would have us believe otherwise, it is naïve in the extreme to downplay the effects of economic and social inequality on student achievement in education. Poverty impacts housing, healthcare, family life and neighborhood safety 'all of which in turn can affect engagement and academic achievement' (Rose, 2006, p. xxiv). From our observations, teachers in the re-engagement programs often went to extraordinary lengths to assist students, to become more financially secure and better connected to community services but they also acknowledged the crucial importance of 'significant others' in supporting their work. In what follows, we will confine our discussion to the role of practitioners and service providers, but we recognize the personal capital that young people possess and importance of existing social networks that contribute to their identity formation (Phillips, 2010). From our conversations with students, it was apparent that parents, grandparents, other family members, friends and peers were often the most significant people in their lives.

Although many of the adults interviewed in our research project were not directly involved in the education of students they did have a connection to these young people through their professional lives in areas such as clinical psychology, maternal health care, youth services, community policing, social welfare and youth housing. In some instances they cooperated closely with schools, and education providers in the provision of counseling services and teaching programs and often had a good working knowledge of the success or otherwise of re-engagement programs. Others had less understanding of what was happening in the education programs but were able to offer insights into the issues confronting young people and the range of community services available to them. Conversations with these individuals confirmed our belief that turning around the damaged lives of young people cannot be achieved solely through schooling. It requires an integrated and collective approach in which the social, economic and cultural resources of communities are directed to improving the lot of the most marginalized. In what follows, we will focus our discussion on issues of student engagement with reference to youth housing, juvenile justice and counseling services.

Youth housing and education

Governments attach a great deal of importance to policies affirming education and school retention as a means of increasing economic productivity and reducing social exclusion. However, as Rowe and Savelsberg (2010) point out, these policies:

> are based on the assumption that all young people have relatively uniform and stable social circumstances, such as supportive parents within a functional domestic context, and fairly secure housing tenure. (p. 36)

This may be true for students from middle-class backgrounds, but in the words of a young informant, 'not everyone has a perfect life' (Smyth, Hattam, et al., 2000, p. 99). According to Chamberlain and MacKenzie, (2004) on any night, there are almost 100,000 Australians who could be categorized as homeless. Nearly half this group is aged under 25 years, and young people aged 12 to 18 make up a quarter of all those who are homeless. Research has found that most teenagers who become homeless while at school will eventually drop out (Australian Housing and Research Institute, 2004). During the course of our research we interviewed several young people who had experienced periods of homelessness. Some lived rough on the streets but more commonly they moved from house to house staying with friends—a phenomenon known as couch surfing. A few managed to secure stop-gap housing in hostels, boarding homes or caravans. As described previously, one of the major priorities for managers of the engagement programs was to find stable accommodation for these students. They did so with the support of community housing officers and youth workers like Noah who works with homeless youth in Federation City.

> **It's hard for young people to focus on schooling when they are 'couch surfing and have no adults in their lives'**
>
> I'm a youth development worker in homelessness. I've been in the job for 12 months and the ones I work with are mostly 18–25 year olds. I do some work with a supported housing service and provide assistance to the homeless. It's hard for young

people to focus on schooling when they are 'couch surfing' and have no adults in their lives. In this situation, education comes a lot further down the track. I work with these kids when they are in a youth housing facility. They register with Uniting Care and they refer them to different services in Federation City. Once they get into housing they tend go well for a while but then they relapse. Often it's because of relationship breakdowns and the young person feels neglected. They are more often than not couples and some with children. Youth homelessness is a problem in Federation City and there's a shortage of accommodation.

The 21-year-olds that I deal with they are looking to get back into education, but regular schooling isn't an option, which makes it difficult for them. The people we deal with often have drug and alcohol problems, mental health issues and so on. We work with general practitioners and other health providers but the main thing is to get them into supportive housing and then take it from there. One of the main issues is mental health—especially anxiety issues. Sometimes they don't take their medication and they need someone to look after them. Also they generally don't have the basic living skills that we take for granted, like how to cook and budget for food. They are inclined to spend all their money on mobile phones. Often these young people are treated poorly by the community so quite a lot of the work we do is raising awareness of youth homelessness as an issue. One of the prevailing views around here is that they are all on drugs and they are all hopeless. From a housing perspective it is quite difficult to overcome this attitude and renting agencies often compound the problem.

From my perspective there are three main things that these young people need. Number one is a stable living environment. Number two, diagnosis and treatment of health issues, and number three, is education. If they aren't getting three meals a day they can't learn. That might be missed in a normal school process because the teachers think they are a pain in the arse kids and they boot them out. Someone said if the kids make it to school it's quite an achievement and they need to be applauded for that. (Extract from a portrait developed from a transcript of an interview with Noah, 24/5/2011)

Juvenile justice and schooling

Young people in crisis often end up in the criminal justice system, an outcome that can be very destructive for their education, employment prospects and life chances. Clearly police have a vested interest in crime prevention, but schools too can reap the benefits when students' education is not disrupted by time out in juvenile detention. In this portrait we gain an insight into a regional crime prevention program initiated by Michelle, a police officer with a special brief for working with youth in a regional center. In cooperation with the coordinator of *Stepping Out* (an alternative education program in Merino Plains) she established a project which sought to build relationships between young people and the police and a better understanding of the law. Michelle highlights the issues confronting young people, the success of her work and the frustrations of working in a policy environment which does not attach a sufficient priority to the provision of an adequately funded and holistic approach to youth services.

'My role is a proactive one'

I work with youth at risk of entering the criminal justice system. My first partnership was with Stepping Out, a re-engagement program for young people in Merino Plains. We came up with a program which was funded by the state government. To begin with we had very strict guidelines for kids entering into the program. We took only those young people who had been disengaged from learning for two years. I worked with the students for one session per week. The incentive was that if they attended regularly they got to go on adventure camps. We wanted them to experience organized adventure activities like caving, surfing, canoeing, and horse riding and all that. Really, it was all about enhancing relationship with police and the flow-on affect of keeping young people out of trouble with the law. The program was successful but after one year funding was no longer available so I wasn't able to continue.

I knew the kids at Stepping Out because of my policing role in schools so I wasn't coming in cold. They saw me as a positive person. My role is essentially a proactive one. The aim is to reduce youth crime by building relationships. I'm usually in uniform but if by request they feel more comfortable with me out of uniform then I don't wear it. Some of the big issues facing young people are drug and alcohol abuse, mental health, break-down in family relationships, lack of parent supervision, and disengagement from school. It is difficult to access any service for young people with the staffing cuts that community health organizations have suffered. If you are in crisis there is nowhere to go. There's a huge gap in mental health and drug dependency services. We do have homelessness but it's not as obvious as you would see in the large cities. You don't see bed rolls and things, but you see kids couch surfing.

We've had some success stories in my Stepping Out program. In the early days we saw one girl through the project and she went on to do art at university. Some are working in supermarkets and some boys are working in the trades. I've worked with Stepping Out kids this year running 7 sessions in things like bullying, property damage, healthy relationships, and so on. The Stepping Out coordinator managed to get some funding to keep it going. Unfortunately, the Police Commissioner got rid of the police-in-schools model and decided to go with the youth model saying that 'at risk' kids weren't in primary schools but I beg to differ. There's no money around for at-risk kids until youth justice—there's a huge gap. When they go to youth justice they then kick in with all the funds for psychologists, drug and alcohol rehabilitation and so on. Another problem is that there is no generalist youth worker in Merino Plains. You've got all these different youth workers doing their own thing in housing, health, etc., but we have no funding for a generalist youth worker. Qualified psychologists are very thin on the ground. You can't just get a kid to see a psychologist. Some kids are put into housing up to aged 21 but they just haven't got the life skills to cope. I think the community views my work in a positive light. As for the Stepping Out kids, they are judged as crooks, trouble makers and so on but from my point of view they are kids that are displaced. <u>They don't fit in.</u> (Extract of a portrait developed from a transcript of an interview with Michelle, 23/5/2011)

Police officers, health workers and youth counselors see aspects of young lives that are less visible to teachers and schools. They may be more aware of the impact of domestic violence, parental neglect, sexual abuse and criminal behavior on kids, and they may have strategies which can work in tandem with school policies to support the education of the most marginalized youth. The pro-active work that Michelle does with students is part of a crime-prevention strategy, but it also has an important education function insofar as it involves students in adventure activities that help to build their self-confidence, team work and social skills.

Youth counseling

All too often outside agencies work at arm's length from schools and students and what they offer is restricted to one-off seminars/workshops or individual counseling programs. In the next portrait we see how Erin, a drug and alcohol counselor, forged a close relationship with the coordinator of the *Stepping Out* program and provided much needed guidance to young people on matters of sexuality, health, and other social issues that are sometimes neglected in schools. Through her ongoing involvement with the program she assisted them to build support networks and a more informed knowledge of their own health and wellbeing.

'Stepping Out *is much more than a school'*

I had developed a good relationship with Kate (the coordinator) and got to know some of the kids through a local youth organization. Kate would phone me and say "One kid is a little off would you come in and see what you can do". The kids are flourishing and the program is fantastic. The first project we ran was an art project with Stepping Out and the art gallery. It was great because the kids got to go into another part of Merino Plains. My relationship has been quite casual. The kids are not daunted to come and see me if they want to. We don't have a generalist youth worker in Merino Plains but in my work I would come across kids that were not in the Stepping Out program and needed counseling.

Stepping Out has so much to offer kids and Kate is like a mother figure to them. I noticed improvements in their self-esteem and communication skills. Initially they don't trust you because you were an adult but that changed with time. Nowadays they start coming in the door where they didn't do that before. One of the other co-workers works at a restaurant, and she has put a few on, and some have gone on to university. Another teacher, Elizabeth, runs a program with the young mums which is invaluable because they haven't had the upbringing that other kids have. They don't know about nutrition and health matters. One of the kids said 'I'll have a baby and I'll get a house'. That really shocked me. She is homeless because her mum pushed her out the door. There are quite a few social problems around here. I've been working a lot with kids who haven't been to school from 13 to 21 years of age. Often it's to do with parents and family structure breakdowns. I was seeing as many as 60–70 kids a year which was much more than I could handle. My workload was supposed to be 12 kids but I was working with 20 at a time and I felt like I was just band aiding.

> I've never had a shortage of kids to see. They talk to me about issues they wouldn't be game to ask their parents. I think they see me more like a big sister and sometimes the tougher person who says to them that's not okay to engage in certain behaviors, that we are not there to be abused or say, it's okay when it isn't. I've had a few kids that ask why unprotected sex isn't okay. I guess too that we are in the same town, and confidentiality needs to be kept. I've probably been used by various schools for different reasons. Sometimes schools threaten the student with me and that makes me feel awful. Even nurses can't do pregnancy tests without telling the parents. Some schools don't give out condoms. To me it's preventative measure and I make sure that all this stuff is there for them to access. What I was doing was hard work because I'm supposed to be doing drug and alcohol counseling but I found myself doing so much other stuff as well. The good thing was my manager trusted me to do my job. Now I've moved on. I needed some space in my life so I'm trying to work out what to do next. (Extract of a portrait developed from a transcript of an interview with Erin, 25/5/2011)

Through their work, Noah, Michelle and Erin created opportunities for some of the most marginalized students to access material and social resources so that they could continue with their education. Without stable housing, health services, and welfare support many would have fallen by the wayside. They also confirmed what students and teachers have to say about these flexible-learning centers, namely that they are places where the social and emotional sides of students' lives are not put on hold. By building relational trust and creating spaces for students to discuss deeply felt concerns these teachers demonstrate a commitment to young people that goes beyond what they experienced in traditional schools.

Concluding remarks

In a keynote address to a regional conference on disadvantage and inequality in education and health, Wyn (2011) remarked that for over a quarter of a century researchers have been documenting the 'failure' of the same groups of Australian youth, notably 'young indigenous people, young people from rural areas and young people living in poverty' (Abstract). However, while techniques for measuring 'failure' with regard to health, education and employment outcomes have improved, a multitude of government programs have not altered existing patterns of disadvantage. We concur with Wyn (2011) that new research and policy frameworks are needed to provide richer knowledge about these issues—frameworks that move away from the idea of risk and deficits to focus on strengths and capabilities of groups and individuals. How different might it be in education if:

- we look beyond the deficit labels attached to the most marginalized youth and view them as being 'at promise' instead of 'at risk' (Swadener & Lubeck, 1995);
- we move away from identifying 'problem students' and look instead to the institutional practices of schools that lead to failure or success (Wyn, 2011);
- we regard all students as having talents and abilities that can contribute to the betterment of society instead of categorizing a small minority of students as gifted on the basis of high academic performance;
- we view the question of school engagement from a student perspective and ask 'how might schools better engage with young people' rather than 'how might young people better engage with schools';
- we shed generic models of schools, curriculum and students in favor of approaches that recognize the distinctiveness of the relationships between schools and communities (Wyn, 2011);
- we conceive of teachers as transformative intellectuals (Giroux, 1985) with a capacity to develop curriculum that is responsive to the lives, aspirations and cultures of young people rather than mere transmitters of skills and knowledge defined by others.

In this and the preceding chapter we have heard from young people and adults about second-chance education programs where there seems to be much less talk of 'youth at risk' and more about opening up choices and opportunities for students in education, employment and community life. We do not believe that these initiatives hold all the answers to improving school retention and student engagement. Indeed, as te Riele (2007) points out, there is a danger that alternative programs may reinforce disadvantages for marginalized youth, especially if they take the form of short-term, therapeutic courses that do not lead to nationally recognized qualifications. On the basis of research in New South Wales, te Riele claims that the most successful programs—the kind we observed in our research sites—have an association with an established institutional unit or school, offer a broad range of educational experiences relevant to young persons' interests and needs, and provide access to educational credentials (te Riele, 2007, p. 59). These programs start from the premise that current educational provisions need to change rather than the young person having to change to fit into the school system. Importantly, they recognize that learning is a multi-dimensional process in which the cognitive domain cannot be isolated from the affective domain that relates to the emotional, social and cultural identities of young people.

We have highlighted the contributions of teachers and 'significant others' in working to reduce educational inequalities but a more holistic and integrated approach to the provision of social, financial and health services is required for young people (and their families) living on the margins of Australian society (Rowe & Savelsberg, 2010). Achieving a greater measure of educational equality in Australia demands a re-thinking of educational policy, but it also requires fundamental changes to the economic and political structures that are the root cause of injustice. These are matters we discuss in chapter 6 where we dare to dream about a fairer and more equitable system of education for all students.

CHAPTER 6

Dreams of a Different World

Changes to Policy and Practice

In this closing chapter we want to start with the proposition that it is not possible to talk about the conditions that lead to educational re-connection and re-engagement of young people with learning, without also taking into account and talking about the conditions that should have been brought into existence in the first place to avoid their dis-engagement. In other words, we need to look at what it is that schools should be doing, as a matter of course *for all students*, not just the 'special' set of ameliorative circumstances that have to be created afterwards to recuperate or rehabilitate those young people who have ended up as 'collateral damage' from an initially unfair system. To put it most directly—the animating question is: how do we create a set of enabling conditions not only for those young people who have 'given up' on school, or more accurately, whom schools and society have 'given up' on by shoving them out of school, that constitute a wholesome set of conditions for learning *for all students*?

What we are tackling here is not dissimilar in many ways to a number of other binaries that are often, by definition, dealt with in isolation from each other, like: equality/inequality; wealth/poverty; racism/whiteness; privileged/underprivileged; elitism/subordination. In each instance, we cannot properly understand how one part of the duality works without also understanding how the other part does its business, especially the part that is in the dominant position.

We want to borrow and build on Lynch and Baker's (2005) useful five key dimensions of an educational equality framework. The indispensable key conditions of equality in education according to Lynch and Baker (2005) are, equality of:

(i) resources
(ii) respect and recognition
(iii) power
(iv) love, care and solidarity
(v) work of teaching and learning. (pp. 132–133)

We believe the reasoning behind this framework (Figure 6.1) goes a long way towards helping us to explain what goes on in educational (re)engagement. The centerpiece of Lynch and Baker's reasoning is the notion of 'equality of condition'—the robust view 'that people should be as equal as possible in relation to the central conditions of their lives...ensuring that everyone has roughly equal prospects of a good life' (p. 132). This involves more than the usual throwaway catchphrase of 'equality of opportunity'. Rather, if equality of access to resources, broadly conceived, becomes our starting point, then it may be possible to see what occurs when some young people become disconnected, dis-engaged, or displaced from school and learning—while others do not—and what transpires in some cases

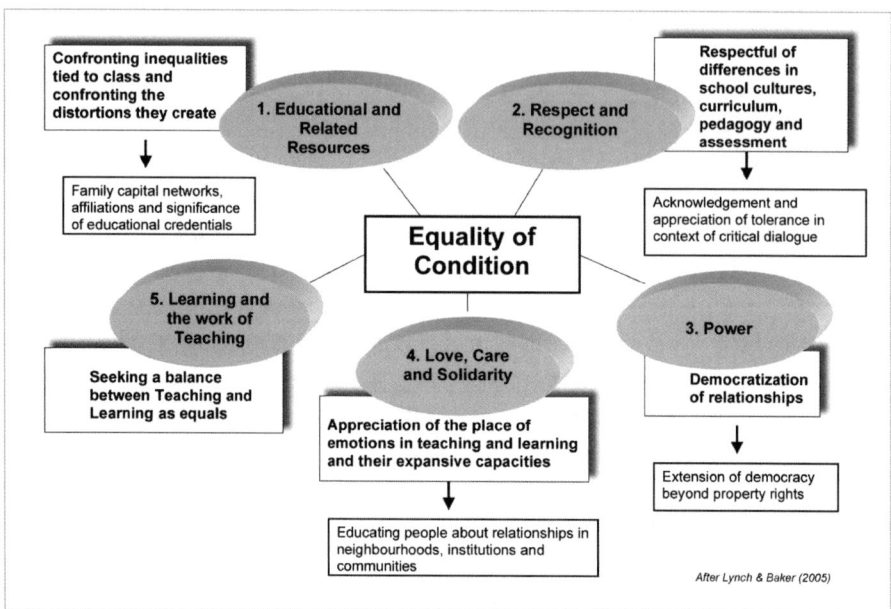

FIGURE 6.1: Five Dimensions of Inequality

where some of the former locate the spaces and conditions in which they can reconnect with learning. Our argument is that issues of engagement within education are not unrelated to matters of equality—across all of Lynch and Baker's dimensions.

An orienting word or two about each of the elements of this 'equality of condition' might be helpful.

(i) Equality of educational and related resources: Lynch and Baker (2005) argue that this involves more than 'economic forms of capital such as income and wealth', important though they are, and that it extends as well to include 'family and social networks and affiliations', in addition to the value social groups attach to 'educational credentials' (p. 132). Lynch and Baker (2005) make the very salient point that no matter what reasons we might think schools exist for, in the end, 'schools are organizational entities with their own priorities and values, a central one of which is survival' (p. 136). How schools end up contributing to social-class inequality occurs through a number of policy relays or regimes.

Selection and admission processes are requiring schools to be increasingly 'market-driven' and seek 'to enroll the most educationally attractive students' (p. 136). This means that 'working class students are more likely to be perceived as a liability [and] a risk to the status of a school in a market-driven system' (p. 136). Savvy middle-class parents who understand how educational markets work, participate through school choice as 'active consumers' (p. 136), while less active (and attractive) working-class parent and students are left behind in residualised schools. Often it is non-middle-class students who have the most difficulty in reconciling their lives, backgrounds and aspirations with that of the middle-class institution of schooling. Working-class children are often the most vocal in speaking back, and as a result are branded recalcitrant and obdurate in their failure to conform to the norms of the school. In a word, they are the students who appear to metaphorically be the most 'untidy', and therefore detract from the idealized market image that schools are seeking to actively cultivate and promote in order to garner market share. They are, therefore, in subtle or not so subtle ways the ones that have to be abandoned or jettisoned in order that schools can maintain their marketable status. What educational markets do, of course, is conceal the process by which the least attractive students, who also happen to be the most educationally disadvantaged, 'are systematically discouraged from entering schools with higher levels of attainment, thereby fostering ghettos of advantage and disadvantage within the school system itself' (Lynch & Baker, 2005, p. 137). Part of the deal here, is to conceal what is really going on, by individualizing the problem around young people and their families, who are argued to be in the state they are in, because they are unprepared to make a commitment to schooling or unwilling to conform to norms established and operated by the invisible hand of the market.

Grouping, tracking and ability processes, are another social-class cloak used to locate and position students. Alleged ability is advanced as a way of appearing to naturalize the way students are benignly sorted and sifted in schools, in ways that in reality are along social-class lines. Students who have already been marginalized and alienated by the abstract and academic ethos of schooling, especially as it is given expression in the middle to latter years of high school, find themselves unceremoniously shunted into vocational tracks that are often highly indicative of the kind of occupational paths already taken by their parents and families.

In an especially controversial revelation in Australia recently (Cervini, 2011), a historian of medical anatomy and anthropology, Ross Jones at University of Sydney, revealed the association of key figures in the eugenics movement in Melbourne, Australia, in the early 1900s as being closely associated with the foundation of the Australian Council for Educational Research (ACER), and its measurement of intelligence—an agency which to this day, still retains its status as the premier national educational testing agency in Australia. Jones goes on to reveal that the origins of vocational tracking in public education in the state of Victoria in the early twentieth century, were associated with the first Director of Education, Frank Tate, a supporter of eugenics, and who brought into existence the process of streaming students into vocational courses at age 12 (see also Jones, 2007, p. 126). As Cervini (2011), interviewing Jones, put it:

> In Victoria, a system of technical schools was established mainly in the northern and western suburbs [of Melbourne—working class areas of high disadvantage] in the 1920s. This was because Tate believed that the working class was genetically fit for vocational education, but not an academic one…In New South Wales, where the head of education was anti-eugenicist, many more students attended state high schools than in Victoria in the 1920s and '30s (p. 15).

In other words, students' fitness for particular forms of schooling appears to have been historically formed on a very dubious basis of ability, which on closer analysis looks more like an attribution of social class than educational aptitude. It is difficult to know with any certainty the extent to which these kind of ideas can be interpellated into processes in other parts of the world, but at least in this context it does bring into question the allegedly 'social-class neutral methods' (Lynch and Baker, 2005, p. 137) by which students are tracked and streamed and who gets to be advantaged or punished as a consequence.

Curriculum and assessment procedures serve to further reinforce these forms of inequality of access to educational resources in the way they prioritize and recognize some forms of literacy—written and 'logical-mathematical capabilities' (Lynch & Baker, 2005, p. 138)—while demeaning or ignoring others, such as students from strongly oral traditions, or vernacular forms of expression and codes that are not recognized in largely Anglo school cultures. Students who experience difficulties in accessing these 'elaborated' codes, as Bernstein (1971) termed them, are deemed 'failures', in a process that is further legitimated by 'pen and paper' forms of testing that are 'often remote from the reality they purport to examine' (Lynch & Baker, 2005, p. 138)— a point repeatedly made to us by the young people in our research who had been (dis)engaged from school. What we have operating here, are not indicators of inferior intelligence, but rather the workings of a system of 'knowledge, capabilities and intelligences that are associated with occupations and statuses that are already privileged in society' (p. 139). What is labeled 'disengagement' and 'disconnection' from learning, while it might appear to be the last step in a long line of frustration, in actuality amounts to the attribution of particular groups who do not fit, to 'subordinated statuses and class positions' (p. 139) in which they are effectively excluded from the benefits of school.

In sum, as Lynch and Baker (2005) put it:

> While social class inequality in education [of which disengagement is a major exemplifying symptom] manifests itself in terms of individual injustice, its origins lie in the institutionalized inequality to access... (p. 139)

...to a wider range of social and relational resources necessary to enable one to participate on equal terms with others.

To summarize, it is clear that students' abilities to engage with and be successful with what is offered by schools is differentially mediated by the extent to which they have access to resources, which can extend considerably beyond what schools and educational systems regard as individual attributes of intelligence, motivation and commitment. In reality, educational engagement and success have much more to do with the presence, or not, of 'institutionalized inequality of access' either directly, or by some proxy, in ways that equate to the capacity of individuals to acquire educational resources 'on equal terms with others' (Lynch & Baker, 2005, p. 139). For example, educational privileging is secured in all kinds of ways including the transactions schools engage in whereby they recognize and reward middle-class parents in return for their continuing patronage. Puncturing and exposing this kind of privileging requires, Lynch and Baker (2005) argue, greater transparency in how decisions are made, and for whom, as well as being open about what constitutes intelligence. In other words, 'opening up the inside life of schools to democratic scrutiny and public challenge' (p. 140), something that requires extreme courage. Likewise, this transparency has to be extended to 'bodies controlling curriculum and syllabus design and assessment procedures' (p. 141)—something powerful and vested interest groups are decidedly reluctant to do.

The necessity for this kind of challenging of 'silencing' and 'devaluation', leads Lynch and Baker (2005) to argue that there needs to be much greater attention to 'the cultural aspects of class politics' to do with 'recognition and respect' (p. 142)—something we would concur with and see as lying at the root of student educational engagement.

(ii) Equality of Respect and Recognition are among the most significant forms of inequality that constitute a major educational impediment for some groups. Absence of recognition and respect, at the institutional level of the school and the educational system, amount to symbolic forms of 'denial' and 'depreciation' that comprise a form of 'cultural imperialism' that renders people 'either invisible, or if visible, subjects them to negative stereotyping and misrecognition' (p. 143). Inequality of respect and recognition, not only devalue, demean and condemn, but they constitute a 'systematic bias' that undermines the very capacity to learn. Learning is, after all, about risk taking, and taking risks requires a degree of trust in a climate where mistakes can be made without being attributed to fugitive notions of 'deficits'.

Silence, invisibility and devaluation can often occur through unthinking heterogeneity, around sexuality, gender, ability and social class—that presumes qualities that may not be present. When there are organizational presumptions about lifestyle or the possession of resources that don't coincide with those of schools, then 'failure' or educational disengagement is likely be mis-recognized and mis-labeled. Indeed, where there is a deeply entrenched inability to recognize and 'name social class inequalities' (Lynch & Baker, 2005, p. 144), for example, there is a pronounced possibility that both teachers and students will 'resort to stereotypes of so-called commonsense', which is really code for 'individualizing responsibility for difference in performance' (p. 144). In our research, young people who were recipients, often labeled this as 'bullying'. The consequence of this lack of a more analytical vocabulary, can have quite devastating consequences for some students.

Systematic bias and subordination of the feminine is an illustration of the perpetuation of what Bourdieu and Passeron (1977) term 'cultural arbitraries', in which education in general is impoverished because of the construction of false dichotomies. An illustration of this can be seen, according to Lynch and Baker (2005) in the misleading separation of supposedly 'rational' aspects of education—those parts that can be measured, calibrated, compared and controlled—

and the 'emotional and affective'—those elements which are neglected, ignored, diminished, pilloried, punished and subordinated. When this occurs, what we have is a form of gendered 'cultural imperialism' that is blind to the emotional aspects of learning and that results in the 'impoverish[ment of] education for all students' (p. 145).

Likewise, in the case of **Segregation and Disability**, there are profound negative effects on learning when people with differences are segregated—what gets to be sedimented is ignorance of differences that can only be properly understood and learned 'on an informal day-to-day basis' (p. 146).

These aspects of inequality of respect and recognition are of a type that places them somewhat more within the reach and control of schools to do something about—which is not to say they are necessarily easy to achieve—in contrast to inequality of resources. The kind of guiding principles Lynch and Baker (2005) proffer are around: (i) inclusion, by which they mean having a day-to-day ethical and empathetic demeanor in creating safe places in which learning about diversity can occur for all; and (ii) ensuring that there is a crucial alignment of curriculum, pedagogy and assessment systems, in the way they give active expression and license to the inclusion of oppressed groups in the way learning is designed in the first place. Our argument is that unless both of these are overtly and explicitly present at both levels, then a likely outcome will be the disenfranchisement, disillusionment, disengagement and detachment of students from schooling—for all of the wrongly attributed reasons.

(iii) Equality of power and the democratization of education. To our way of thinking, and from what consistently emerged from the young people in our study who conveyed a profound sense of what it meant to have been through disengagement from schools, and emerged out the other side in a re-invented form, from their vantage point this has often been the most salient form of inequality. Repeatedly, they told us, that not having ownership of their learning was the most debilitating aspect they encountered. Another way of putting this was that young people felt that everyone else had power over their learning and that the result for them was 'exclusion, marginalization, trivialization and misrepresentation' (Lynch & Baker, 2005, p. 148) of what was really transpiring in their lives. The way young people in our study put it was that they profoundly experienced power 'relationally'—which is to say, they felt it in the way they were dealt with impersonally, sorted, sifted, measured, calibrated, categorized and in the end hierarchically subordinated. They spoke directly and often quite emotionally about the way power was visited upon them in institutionalized and impersonal ways—around seemingly petty and infantile matters of dress codes, deportment, punctuality, substance use, and the like—all of which were elevated in importance above that of quality

human relationships, often with institutionalized policies like that around bullying, being blatantly ignored by teachers and schools.

Democratization of educational relations was one of the most consistent themes emerging from our research with young people. They continually told us how they lived relational lives in all kinds of ways, even on occasions within seemingly quite disconnected and isolated settings. As Turkle (2011) put it in the title of her book, it is often a case of young people being *Alone Together*—reference to the increasingly digitally connected nature of young lives. Much of the dialogue young people are engaging in with others, is much more horizontal than the hierarchical relational arrangements they experience in schools. As Lynch and Lodge (2002) have found, young people are seeking and requiring 'greater democratization of schooling, both at the organizational and at the classroom levels' (p. 165). One of the reasons for this is that 'it is not surprising given that many young people are working part-time while at school' (Lynch & Lodge, 2002, p. 165), and as a consequence, they are inhabiting environments *beyond school* that treat them with maturity and in ways that are less dependent on adult authority. In sum, young people 'often exercise a high level of autonomy in relation both to work and leisure outside of school, an autonomy that is greatly facilitated by their relative financial independence' (p. 165). None of this is especially new, but as Lodge and Lynch (2000) reiterate, 'the core relationship of the school institution is a power based one in which young people are structurally defined as subordinate to adults' (p. 46). In other words, power relationships continue to be 'at the center of schooling from the perspective of young people' (p. 46). Little wonder there is likely to be what Freebody, Ludwig and Gunn (1995) call 'interactive trouble' (p. 297)—a situation where schools are defining one reality for young people, while young people themselves are creating, inhabiting and experiencing a very different one *beyond school*.

Challenging and changing these inegalitarian relationships is not likely to be an easy task, requiring as Lynch and Baker (2005) indicate, changes at the level of teacher-student relationships, as well as at the level of 'democratizing the wider set of relations within which schools exist' (p. 150)—which is to say, the way in which teachers are treated with respect at the policy level, the way in which communities are trusted as having something worthwhile to say, and the way the whole educational planning process is handled by the state in a way that indicates the value attached to professional judgment. Without changes at that wider level, changes at the level of relationships in classrooms and schools between teachers and students are unlikely to be sustainable. Overlay this with groups of young people who come from contexts of poverty where they have repeatedly been subjected to marginalization, exclusion, alienation and 'failure', and the complexities become considerably magnified. The wider set of injustices that have shaped and formed young lives more generally, have to be democratized along with relationships inside schools, if the 'intrinsic' value of education is to be fully realized for these young people.

(iv) Equality of love, care and solidarity. The fourth element of Lynch and Baker's (2005) equality framework that bears on what we have researched in this book addresses what lies at the crucial heart of teachers' work—the undeniably emotional nature of that work (p. 150), that is about genuinely caring for students, their lives, their families, their hopes and aspirations for the future, and doing this in a context in which 'emotional capabilities' (p. 153) can only really flourish through interdependency in relations with other people. It is also more than that. Solidarity also implies resort to collective relationships that may have to be used to usurp entrenched unjust practices. Connell (1993) put this view about the social, emotional and relational nature of teaching as a social practice like this:

> Being a teacher is not just a matter of having a body of knowledge and a capacity to control a classroom. That could be done by a computer with a cattle-prod. Just as important, being a teacher means being able to establish human relations with the people being taught. Learning is a full-blooded, human social process, and so is teaching. Teaching involves emotions as much as it involves pure reasoning.
>
> The emotional dimension of teaching has not been much researched, but in my view is extremely important. Teachers establish relations with students through their emotions, through sympathy, interest, surprise, boredom, sense of humor, sometimes anger and annoyance. School teaching, indeed, is one of the most emotionally demanding jobs (p. 63)...
>
> Good teachers in disadvantaged schools regularly perform astonishing (and unheralded) feats of human relations, overcoming age, class and ethnic barriers, breaking through resentment, suspicions and fears, to establish workable educational relationships (p. 63).

When we deny, belittle or diminish the importance of the relational nature of teachers' work, then we effectively distort or deform it. When we allow this to happen, or fail to robustly challenge it, then we become implicated in the degradation of that work and complicit in allowing it to be represented as a fake representation or facsimile of the real thing. As we have shown repeatedly though our earlier body of research (Smyth, 1991; Smyth & Shacklock, 1998; Smyth et al., 2000; Smyth, Dow, Hattam, Reid & Shacklock, 2000; Smyth, 2001; Smyth & Hattam et al., 2004; Smyth & McInerney, 2007; Smyth, Angus, Down & McInerney, 2008), teaching is profoundly relational work that occurs quintessentially in activist and solidarity ways (Smyth, Angus, Down & McInerney, 2009) in and through the *'relational school'* (Smyth, Down & McInerney, 2010).

While a rationalist, positivist, masculinist and macho-military/corporatist-driven world may seem to be a sign of strength, and celebrating feminine qualities like 'love', 'care' and 'emotions' a sign of weakness, the existential reality is that these are the defining qualities of good teaching—and when they are absent, frustrated from being allowed to come into existence, or laminated over by what are considered to be more muscular targets, deliverables, league tables, and outcomes, then the inevitable result is a lack of relational learning and student detachment leading to rejection of the whole educational edifice—as we have graphically illustrated in the young lives represented in this book.

Lynch and Baker (2005) argue that when we 'neglect the emotions' (p. 151), and take a limited view that learning is only about the 'intellect', then we run the enormous risk that student growth is likely to be seriously impaired because of the absence of 'emotional support and care in their personal lives'. In other words, despite what we are repeatedly told by the media and its complicit predatory consumption industry, people are not stand-alone profit and loss cost-centers: 'people live their lives in relations of dependency and independency' (p. 153). The consequence of such disregard, is the enhanced likelihood of 'opting out of school' (p. 152). What is required instead, according to Lynch and Baker (2005), is 'a language and a space so that students and teachers have a language and a space to talk about their feelings' (p. 153), unlike what we found in our study entitled *Listen to Me, I'm Leaving* (Smyth et al., 2000) where young people reported being effectively told to park their lives and emotions at the school gate!

(v) Equality of work and learning is in a sense, the amalgam of how all of these other forms of equality of condition come together both to provide access to resources in the future for young people in their lives, but also as Baker et al., (2009) put it, 'working and learning as equals' (p. 39) which is really about the intrinsic satisfaction that ought to attach to both work and learning. Where burdens of these are inequitably distributed, and *teaching* is defined exclusively as teachers' work, and *learning* as students' work, then we have a problematic inequality.

In our case of young people who have become detached, dissociated, or disconnected from school, then learning has become a relational burden that they are not prepared to endure. In other words, they are not prepared to make the social and emotional investment in forming the relationships necessary for learning to occur. The price of the conditions put upon them is considered to be too high, and they have chosen to put their energies, emotions and efforts elsewhere in doing their identity work—often to their detriment, in the short term, of substance abuse, delinquency, criminality, or the like, as well as in the long term, of being unable to live a rewarding life. Schools, on the other hand, seem not to have the real interests of students in mind when they demand such a high price of compliance to petty rules and regulations that young people consider have no relationship to what is required to become an educated person.

When young people re-engage with learning, after having exiled themselves, or having been rendered so because of institutional intolerance or indifference, then what these young people are effectively doing is re-writing the conditions of their learning relationships—along more equitable and democratic lines.

What are we to make of this? —educational policy, practice and research

We can best draw our account of what we have attempted here in terms of giving another 'reading' to some young lives, to some kind of uneasy closure, by reflecting for a few moments on some of the terrain we have traversed, both methodologically and substantively.

At the outset, in chapter 2, we stepped out and made our position crystal clear—that we regarded it as an ethical imperative to 'speak the unpleasant' (Chavez & O'Donnell, 1998) in respect of what is happening to young lives, much of it being orchestrated by global forces and tendencies that are warehoused through some highly questionable approaches being inflicted on schools and young people.

Secondly, in chapter 3, we dealt with what we see as the 'messy' approach of trying to peer behind the mask and veil of how power works, and for whom, and the effects. What we then proceeded to do, in chapters 4 and 5, was to listen to the storylines from the young people, the adults who worked with them as educators, and significant others who were witnesses to the effects—and give some amplification to these through a process of portraiture. In and through the process of our fieldwork and analysis, although we did not dwell on it at great length, we regard ourselves as enacting what Sloan (2009) has referred to as 'doing theory critically' (pp. 319–334)—which is to say:

> …exposing and being suspicious of the assumptions that fuel theory, especially when these assumptions reflect power relations and social processes that foster oppression or exclusion…
>
> …questioning the analytic move that isolates individuals from their life contexts in order to explain their behavior solely in terms of internal or immediate situational factors…
>
> …looking hard for what has been hidden by or left out of concepts that purport to explain a certain phenomenon…or covers up…the essence of something (p. 324).

Consistent with our 'up front' and advocacy style of research that is attentive and attuned to capturing the lives, experiences, perspectives, hope and aspirations of those who are normally excluded, and using these to 'speak back' to injustice—we offer the following as a kind of manifesto about what needs to change if young people like these are to have a hope of a better life:

- The old muscular *pedagogy of disconnection* script is not working—it is thoroughly discredited, and the evidence of increasing exclusion is on display for all to see—we need to be better at marshalling the evidence of what is not working and reflecting it back into the public domain.
- We need a new and invigorated 'connectionist' social imaginary (Taylor, 2007)—what we might term a *pedagogy of reconnection*, that comes from the lives and experiences of informants in the kind of study we have conducted here.
- We need to demonstrate how the *'local solutions'* developed in this study *resonate with similar studies done elsewhere* of programs and approaches that look like what we have described.
- We need to be innovative and creative in finding ways of developing coalitions and alliances to discredit and ultimately dislodge the *deficit forms of thinking* and the *damaging neoliberal model* that dominates at the moment.
- We need to be better at *working at the local level with communities* to make alternatives for young people an *actually existing reality*.
- To do this, we will need to embark on *activist educational and community reform approaches that reclaim the public spaces* for debate and discussion of the alternatives.
- We need to be indignant that current *individualized and victim-blaming approaches* constitute a 'thin' and *flawed pathological approach* to the problems confronting young lives, that denies social, political and economic complexity. We need to confront and name one-dimensional intervention approaches, that purport to be able to *break cycles of disadvantage and poverty* and *mend the broken links of social exclusion and isolation*.
- We need to reveal how the much more complex sets of forces and flows operating nationally and internationally, present as *interferences and obstacles* to education and learning for young people in some contexts.
- We need to find the *public spaces and places in which to proclaim* the virtues of alternative educational arrangements and experiences that work for the most excluded young people, and insist that these are acknowledged and properly resourced.

In the end, rather than thinking of all this as bringing on a full-frontal revolution, we need to be smarter at articulating and gaining support though *a soft revolution* for a *more socially just alternative* for young people, and showing its demonstrable benefits over dominant neoliberal approaches.

Appendix

Summary of Student Interviews and Re-engagement Programs

Program	Affiliation	Male	Female	Total
Connexions Young Parent Group	Federation City High School	2	16	18
Beyond School	Federation City West Community College	10	2	12
Satellite Applied Learning Certificate	Federation City South High School	8	8	16
Connexions Work	Federation City High School	4	3	7
Connexions Education	Federation City High School	3	6	9
Youth Pathways	Crystal Springs High School	1	2	3
Satellite Applied Learning Certificate	Crystal Springs High School	0	2	2
Stepping Out	Merino Plains High School	8	16	24
Satellite Applied Learning Certificate	Merino Plains High School	3	6	9
TOTALS		39	61	100

References

Anderson, G. (1989). Critical ethnography in education: Origins, current status, and new directions. *Review of Educational Research, 59*(3), 249–270.

Anyon, J. (2009). *Theory and Educational Research: Toward Critical Social Explanation*. New York: Routledge.

Australian Bureau of Statistics. (2010). *Births Australia 2009 Number 3301.0*. Canberra.

Australian Housing and Research Institute (AHURI). (2004). *School Students Who Are Homeless: Finding Solutions Research and Policy Bulletin* (Vol. 49). Melbourne: AHURI.

Ayers, W. (2004). *Teaching Towards Freedom: Moral Commitment and Ethical Action in the Classroom*. Boston: Beacon Press.

Bailey, C. (2008). Public ethnography. In S. Hesse-Biber & P. Leary (Eds.), *Handbook of Emergent Methods* (pp. 265–281). New York: Guilford Press.

Baker, J., Lynch, K., Cantillon, S., & Walsh, J. (2009 Second Edition). *Equality: From Theory to Action*. Basingstoke: Palgrave Macmillan.

Bernstein, B. (1971). On the classification and framing of educational knowledge. In M. Young (Ed.), *Knowledge and Control: New Directions for the Sociology of Knowledge* (pp. 19–46). London: Collier-Macmillan.

Bessant, J. (2007). The value of ethnographic research: University students and financial hardship. *Children Australia, 32*(4), 25–34.

Beutel, D. (2010). The nature of teacher-student interactions: A phenomenographic study. *The Australian Educational Researcher, 37*(2), 77–91.

Blum, R. (2005). A case for school connectedness. *The Adolescent Learner, 62*(7), 16–20.

Bourdieu, P., & Passeron, J. (1977). *Reproduction in Education, Society and Culture*. Beverly Hills, CA: Sage Publications.

Brown, P. (1987). *Schooling Ordinary Kids: Unemployment and New Vocationalism*. London: Tavistock.

Bryk, A., & Schneider, B. (2002). *Trust in Schools: A Core Resource for Improvement*. New York: Russell Sage Foundation.

Burgess, R. (1988). Conversations with a purpose: The ethnographic interview in educational research. In R. Burgess (Ed.), *Studies in Qualitative Methodology, Volume 1* (pp. 137–155), Greenwich, CT: JAI Press.

Camus, A. (1948). *The Plague*. New York: Vintage.

Carspecken, P., & Apple, M. (1992). Critical qualitative research: Theory, methodology and practice. In M. L. Compte, W. Millroy & J. Preissle (Eds.), *The Handbook of Qualitative Research in Education* (pp. 507–553). San Diego: Academic Press.

Cervini, E. (2011, 13 September). A theory out of the darkness. *The Age*, p. 15.

Chamberlain, C., & MacKenzie, D. (2004). *Youth Homelessness: Four Proposals*. Melbourne: Australian Housing and Research Institute.

Chapman, T. (2005). Expressions of "voice" in portraiture. *Qualitative Inquiry, 11*(1), 27–51.

Chavez, R., & O'Donnell, J. (Eds.). (1998). *Speaking the Unpleasant: The Politics of (non) Engagement in the Multicultural Education Terrain*. Albany: State University of New York Press.

Collins. (2001). *Collins Australian Concise Dictionary*. Glasgow: HarperCollins.

Connell, B. (1993). *Schools and Social Justice*. Toronto: Our Schools/Our Selves Education Foundation.

Costello, T. (1997). Some values are free. *The Age*(16 January), 15.

Darling-Hammond, L. (1997). *The Right to Learn: A Blueprint for Creating Schools that Work*. San Francisco: Jossey-Bass.

Davis, D. (Ed.). (2004). *You Look Too Young to Be a Mom: Teen Mothers Speak Out on Love, Learning and Success*. New York: Perigee Books

Delpit, L. (1995). *Other People's Children: Cultural Conflicts in the Classroom*. New York: The New Press.

Denzin, N. (2008). The new paradigm dialogs and qualitative inquiry. *International Journal of Qualitative Studies in Education, 21*(4), 315–325.

Department of Education and Early Childhood Development. (2009). *Guidelines for the Delivery of Community VCAL*. Melbourne: DEECD.

Department of Education and Early Childhood Development. (2010). *Pathways to Re-engagement through Flexible Learning Options: A Policy Direction for Consultation*. Melbourne: Student Wellbeing Division, DEECD.

Dewey, J. (2001). *The School and Society and the Child and the Curriculum*. New York: Dover.

Dixon, A., Chapman, T., & Hill, D. (2005). Research as aesthetic process: Extending the portraiture methodology. *Qualitative Inquiry, 11*(1), 16–26.

Duffy, K. (1995). *Social Exclusion and Human Dignity in Europe. Report for the Steering Committee on Social Policy, Council on Europe*. Strasbourg.

Dusseldorp Skills Forum. (2007). *It's Crunch Time: Raising Youth Engagement and Attainment*. Sydney: Dusseldorp Skills Forum.

References

Ennew, J. (2000). *How Can We Define Citizenship in Childhood?* (Vol. 109, 12): Working Paper Series, Harvard Center for Population and Development Studies Harvard School of Public Health.

Fine, M., & Vanderslice, V. (1992). Qualitative activist research: Reflections on methods and politics. In E. Posavac (Ed.), *Methodological Issues in Applied Social Psychology* (pp. 199–218). New York: Plenum.

Fine, M., & Weis, L. (1998). Writing the 'wrongs' of fieldwork: Confronting our own research/writing dilemmas in urban ethnographies. In G. Shacklock & J. Smyth (Eds.), *Being Reflexive in Critical Educational and Social Research* (pp. 13–35). London: Falmer Press.

Fitzgerald, T. (2009). Comforting the afflicted or afflicting the comfortable? Challenges for researchers in education and health. Paper presented at the Addressing Disadvantage and Inequality in Education and Health Research Conference, University of Ballarat.

Foley, D. (2002). Critical ethnography: The reflexive turn. *International Journal of Qualitative Studies in Education, 15*(4), 469–490.

Foucault, M. (1977). *Discipline and Punish: The Birth of the Prison.* (A. Sheridan Trans.) Harmondsworth: Penguin.

Freebody, P., Ludwig, C., & Gunn, S. (1995). *Everyday Literacy Practices in and out of Schools in Low Socio-economic Urban Communities* (Vol. 1). Melbourne: Curriculum Corporation.

Giroux, H. (1985). Teachers as transformative intellectuals. *Social Education, 49*(5), 376–379.

Giroux, H. (1996). *Fugitive Cultures: Race, Violence and Youth.* New York: Routledge.

Giroux, H. (2006). *The Giroux Reader.* Boulder, CO: Paradigm.

Goodman, J. (1998). Ideology and critique. In G. Shacklock & J. Smyth (Eds.), *Being Reflexive in Critical Educational and Social Research* (pp. 50–66). London: Falmer Press.

Green, N. (2006). Everyday life in distance education: One family's home schooling experience. *Distance Education, 27*(1), 27–44.

Griffiths, M. (2009). Critical approaches in qualitative educational research <http://www.bera.ac.uk/critical-approaches-in-qualitative-educational-research> Accessed online 20/1/2011.

Head, S. (1996). The new, ruthless economy. *New York Review of Books*, February, 47–52.

Hickling-Hudson, H. (2009). Southern Theory and its dynamics for postcolonial education. In R. Coloma (Ed.), *Postcolonial Challenges in Education.* New York: Peter Lang Publishing.

Hinson, G. (1999). "You've got to include an invitation": Engaged reciprocity and negotiated purpose in collaborative ethnography. Paper presented at the 98th Annual Meeting of the American Anthropological Association, Chicago: Illinois.

Hutchby, I., & Moran-Ellis, J. (1998). *Children and Social Competence.* London: Falmer Press.

Jones, R. (2007). *Humanity's Mirror: 150 Years of Anatomy in Melbourne.* Melbourne: Haddington Press.

Kincheloe, J., & Steinberg, S. (Eds.). (1998). *Unauthorized Methods: Strategies for Critical Teaching.* New York: Routledge.

Kozol, J. (1992). *Savage Inequalities: Children in America's Schools.* New York: Harper Perennial.

Kozol, J. (2006). *Rachel and Her Children: Homeless Families in America*. New York: Three Rivers Press.

Lather, P. (1986). Research as praxis. *Harvard Educational Review, 56*(3), 252–277.

Lather, P. (1995). The validity of angels: Interpretive and textual strategies in researching the lives of women with HIV/AIDS. *Qualitative Inquiry, 1*(1), 41–68.

Lawrence-Lightfoot, S. (1986). On goodness in schools: Themes of empowerment. *Peabody Journal of Education, 63*(2), 9–20.

Lawrence-Lightfoot, S. (2009). Foreword. In K. Olson. *Wounded by School: Recapturing the Joy in Learning and Standing Up to Old School Culture*, pp. xi–xvi. New York & London.

Lawrence-Lightfoot, S., & Davis, J. (1997). *The Art and Science of Portraiture*. San Francisco: Jossey-Bass.

Lodge, A., & Lynch, K. (2000). Power: A central educational relationship. *Irish Educational Studies, 19*, 46–68.

Lynch, K., & Baker, J. (2005). Equality in education: An equality of condition perspective. *Theory and Research in Education, 3*(2), 131–164.

Lynch, K., & Lodge, A. (2002). *Equality and Power in Schools; Redistribution, Recognition and Representation*. London: Routledge/Falmer.

Madison, D. (2005). *Critical Ethnography: Methods, Ethics and Performance*. Thousand Oaks, CA: Sage.

Millei, Z. (2010). Is it (still) useful to think about classroom discipline as control? An examination of the problem of discipline. In Z. Millei, T. Griffiths & R. Parkes (Eds.), *Re-theorizing Discipline: Problems, Politics and Possibilities* (pp. 13–26). New York: Peter Lang.

Mills, C. W. (1970 [1959]). *The Sociological Imagination*. Harmondsworth: Penguin.

Mills, M., & McGregor, C. (2010). *Re-engaging Students in Education: Success Factors in Alternative Schools*. West End, Queensland: Youth Affairs Network, Queensland.

Moore, B. (1993). The politics of victim construction. Paper presented at the Australian Studies Association Conference 'Curriculum in Profile', Adelaide.

Morrow, V. (2005). Social capital, community involvement and community cohesion in England: A space for children and young people? *Journal of Social Sciences, 9* (Special Issue), 57–69.

Nagge, J. (1932). Regarding the law of parsimony. *Journal of Genetic Psychology, 41*, 492–494.

Nagle, J. (2001). *Voices from the Margins: The Stories of Vocational High School Students*. New York: Peter Lang Publishing.

Noguera, P. (1995). Preventing and producing violence: A critical analysis of responses to school violence. *Harvard Educational Review, 65*(2), 189–213.

Olson, K. (2009). *Wounded by School: Recapturing the Joy in Learning and Standing up to the Old School Culture*. New York: Teachers College Press.

Osterman, K. (2000). Students' need for belonging in the school community. *Review of Educational Research, 70*(3), 323–367.

Palmer, P. (2007). *The Courage to Teach: Exploring the Inner Landscape of a Teacher's Life*. San Francisco: Jossey-Bass.

References

Payne, R. (1998 [2005]). *Framework for Understanding Poverty*. Highlands, TX: Aha Process Inc.

Phillips, R. (2010). Initiatives to support disadvantaged young people: Enhancing social capital and acknowledging personal capital. *Journal of Youth Studies, 13*(4), 498–504.

Pittaway, S. (2005). Legitimate voices: Teen mothers and education. Paper presented at the 9th Annual Australian Institute of Family Studies Conference, Melbourne.

Postman, N. (1979). *Teaching as a Conserving Activity*. New York: A Delta Book.

Prosser, B., Lucas, B., & Reid, A. (Eds.). (2010). *Connecting Lives and Learning: Renewing Pedagogy in the Middle Years*. Kent Town, South Australia: Wakefield Press.

Ravitch, D. (2010). *The Death and Life of the American School System: How Testing and Choice Are Undermining Education*. Philadelphia: Basic Books.

Rose, M. (2006). *Possible Lives: The Promise of Public Education in America*. New York: Penguin Books.

Rowe, P., & Savelsberg, H. (2010). How are young peoples' experiences of 'home' affecting their engagement with schooling and community? *Youth Studies Australia, 29*(3), 36–42.

Ryan, W. (1976). *Blaming the Victim*. New York: Vintage Books.

Sen, A. (1999). *Development as Freedom*. Oxford: Oxford University Press.

Shor, I. (1996). *When Students Have Power: Negotiating Authority in a Critical Pedagogy*. Chicago: University of Chicago Press.

Sibley, D. (1995). *Geographies of Exclusion: Society and Difference in the West*. London & New York: Routledge.

Sibley, D. (1998). Problematizing exclusion: reflections on space, difference and knowledge. *International Planning Studies, 3*(1), 93–100.

Sloan, T. (2009). Doing theory. In D. Fox, I. Prilleltensky & S. Austin (Eds.), *Critical Psychology: An Introduction* (pp. 319–334). London: Sage Publications.

Smyth, J. (1991). *Teachers as Collaborative Learners: Challenging Dominant Forms of Supervision*. London: Open University Press.

Smyth, J. (2001). *Critical Politics of Teachers' Work: An Australian Perspective*. New York: Peter Lang Publishing.

Smyth, J. (2006). Researching teachers working with young adolescents: Implications for ethnographic research. *Ethnography and Education, 1*(1), 31–51.

Smyth, J. (2010). Young people speaking back from the margins. *Canada Education, 50*(5).

Smyth, J., Angus, L., Down, B., & McInerney, P. (2008). *Critically Engaged Learning: Connecting to Young Lives*. New York: Peter Lang Publishing.

Smyth, J., Angus, L., Down, B., & McInerney, P. (2009). *Activist and Socially Critical School and Community Renewal: Social Justice in Exploitative Times*. Rotterdam, The Netherlands: Sense Publishers.

Smyth, J., Dow, A., Hattam, R., Reid, A., & Shacklock, G. (2000). *Teachers' Work in a Globalising Economy*. London & New York: Falmer Press.

Smyth, J., Down, B., & McInerney, P. (2010). *'Hanging in with Kids' in Tough Times: Engagement in Contexts of Educational Disadvantage in the Relational School.* New York: Peter Lang Publishing.

Smyth, J., Hattam, R., Cannon, J., Edwards, J., Wilson, N., & Wurst, S. (2000). *Listen to Me, I'm Leaving: Early School Leaving in South Australian Secondary Schools.* Adelaide: Flinders Institute for the Study of Teaching; Department of Employment, Education and Training; and Senior Secondary Assessment Board of South Australia.

Smyth, J., Hattam, R., with Cannon, J., Edwards, J., Wilson, N., & Wurst, S. (2004). *'Dropping Out', Drifting Off, Being Excluded: Becoming Somebody Without School.* New York: Peter Lang Publishing.

Smyth, J., & McInerney, P. (2007). *Teachers in the Middle: Reclaiming the Wasteland of the Adolescent Years of Schooling.* New York: Peter Lang.

Smyth, J., & McInerney, P. (2011 (in press)). Whose side are you on? Advocacy ethnography: Some methodological aspects of narrative portraits of disadvantaged young people in socially critical research. *International Journal of Qualitative Studies in Education.*

Smyth, J., & Shacklock, G. (1998). *Remaking Teaching: Ideology, Policy and Practice.* London & New York: Routledge.

Stake, R. (1998). Case studies. In N. Denzin & Y. Lincoln (Eds.), *Strategies of Qualitative Inquiry* (pp. 86–109). Thousand Oaks, CA: Sage.

Swadener, B. (1990). Children and families 'at risk': Etiology, critique and alternative paradigms. *Educational Foundations,* 4(Fall), 17–39.

Swadener, B., & Lubeck, S. (1995). The social construction of children and families "at risk": An introduction. In B. Swadener & S. Lubeck (Eds.), *Children and Families at Promise* (pp. 1–14). Albany: State University of New York Press.

Taylor, C. (2007). Cultures of democracy and citizen efficacy. *Public Culture,* 19(1), 117–150.

te Riele, K. (2007). Educational alternatives for marginalized youth. *The Australian Educational Researcher,* 34(3), 53–68.

te Riele, K. (2011). Raising educational attainment: How young peoples' experiences speak to the compact with young Australians. *Critical Studies in Education,* 52(1), 93–109.

Teese, R., & Polesel, J. (2003). *Undemocratic Schooling: Equity and Quality in Mass Secondary Education in Australia.* Carlton, Victoria: Melbourne University Press.

Thiem, C. (2009). Thinking through education: The geographies of contemporary educational restructuring. *Progress in Human Geography,* 33(2), 154–173.

Turkle, S. (2011). *Alone Together: Why We Expect More from Technology and Less from Each Other.* New York: Perseus Books.

Valencia, R. (Ed.). (1997). *The Evolution of Deficit Thinking. Educational Thought and Practice.* London: Falmer Press.

Valencia, R. (2010). *Dismantling Contemporary Deficit Thinking: Educational Thought and Practice.* New York: Routledge.

Van Maanen, J. (2011). Ethnography as work: Some rules of engagement. *Journal of Management Studies,* 48(1), 218–234.

Vanderbeck, R., & Dunkley, C. (2004). Introduction: Geographies of exclusion, inclusion and belonging in young lives. *Children's Geographies, 2*(2), 177–183.

Walford, G. (2009). For ethnography. *Ethnography and Education, 4*(3), 271–282.

Weiss, R. (1994). *Learning from Strangers: The Art and Method of Qualitative Interview Studies.* New York: Free Press.

Wexler, P. (1992). *Becoming Somebody: Toward a Social Psychology of School.* London: Falmer Press.

White, R., & Wyn, J. (1998). Youth agency and social context. *Journal of Sociology, 34*(3), 314–327.

Willis, P. (1977). *Learning to Labor: How Working Class Kids Get Working Class Jobs.* Westmead, England: Gower.

Willis, P., & Trondman, M. (2000). Manifesto for ethnography. *Ethnography, 1*(1), 5–16.

Wingspread Conference Participants. (2004). Wingspread Declaration. *Journal of School Health, 74*(7), 231–234.

Wrigley, T. (2007). Rethinking education in an era of globalisation. *Journal for Critical Education Policy Studies, 5*(2), 1–14.

Wyn, J. (2007). Learning to 'become somebody well': Challenges for educational policy. *Australian Educational Researcher, 34*(3), 35–52.

Wyn, J. (2011, October 2011). Researching disadvantage and inequality in the context of ERA and CRN. Paper presented at the Addressing Disadvantage and Inequality in Education and Health conference, University of Ballarat, Victoria.

Yardley, E. (2008). Teenage mothers' experience of stigma. *Journal of Youth Studies, 11*(6), 671–684.

Zaidi, A. (1996). The Rochester Renaissance Plan: A corporate farewell to the imagination. Unpublished Manuscript.

Zyngier, D. (2008). (Re)conceptualising connectedness as a pedagogy of engagement. Paper presented at the Australian Association of Research in Education Annual Conference, Brisbane.

Zyngier, D. (2010). *Engaging Pedagogies and Pedagogues: Examining Student Engagement in Action.* Koln, Germany: Lambert Academic Publishing.

Subject Index

A

ability, 52, 60, 76, 80, 98
    grouping, 104-106
Aboriginal, 61
abstract and academic forms of knowledge, 20, 23, 89
academic/vocational divide, 23
accountability standards, 2, 17, 41
active
    agents, 11, 35, 79
    informed participants, 3, 18
activist
    educational and community reform, 109, 112
    research, 35
adult
    authority, 20, 108
    perspectives, 12, 80
advocacy, 112
    ethnography, 35
    research, 4, 29, 33–36
agency, 15, 16, 31, 35, 36, 40, 42, 46, 48–50, 52, 56, 77, 104
alienated, 2, 4, 7, 16, 34, 37, 42, 56, 83, 104, 108
alignment of curriculum, 107
Anglo school cultures, 105
antiwar movement, 13
aspirations, 1, 12, 13, 18, 20, 28, 31, 36, 41, 54, 63, 66, 74, 77, 89, 103, 109, 112
at risk, 4, 20, 23, 30, 35, 43, 47, 50, 62, 63, 80, 81, 94, 95, 98
Australia, 29, 34, 39, 42–44, 61, 63, 99, 104
Australian Council for Educational Research, 104
authoritarian culture of high schools, 72
authorized methods, 83
autonomy, 20, 34, 108

B

basics, 15, 47, 62, 82, 93
Becoming Somebody, 37, 48, 49, 51
being in control, 54, 55, 66
belonging, 19, 47, 48, 56
beyond school, 108
blame, 8, 11, 17, 19, 20–22, 25, 36, 112
bonding, 37
boundaries, 10, 16, 56, 69, 90
bullying, 18, 37, 50, 56, 60, 69, 95, 105

bureaucratic tradition, 83
busy work, 47

C

calibrated, 74, 106, 107
'can do' policy, 10
capabilities, 66, 105, 109
capacities
    to speak, 77
    of young people, 41
care, 37, 45, 47, 48, 57, 66, 77, 81, 83, 86, 102, 109, 110
catalogue of damages, 13
Centrelink, 62, 73
charter schools, 25
choice, 9, 11, 12, 32, 38, 49, 51, 52, 54, 61, 63, 64, 66, 72, 74, 90, 98, 103
codes of conduct, 90
cognitive strategies, absence of, 22
collaboration, 80, 87
collaborative learning, 46
collateral damage, 4, 23, 101
collective relationships, 109
commodification, 17
community
    building activities, 48
    engagement, 30
compassionate places, 77
competitive global economy, 9
complex web of connections, 87
complexity of the school, 13
compliance, 18, 20, 50, 56, 110
conflict resolution, 61
connectedness, 5, 32, 43, 47, 48, 87
connecting
    to learning, 66
    to young lives, 81, 87
control
    over students, 18, 69, 70
    of teachers' work, 10, 84
conviction, 36, 52
couch surfing, 92, 93, 95
courage, 4, 23, 24, 28, 32, 35, 36, 42, 50, 63–65, 77, 79, 83, 85, 103, 106

crime prevention, 94, 95
criminal activity, 52
criminal justice system, 94
criminality, 17, 110
criminalization of young people, 17, 19
crisis of youth, 49
critical
    ethnography, 31, 34, 35
    qualitative research, 28
    social theory, 37
critiques of contemporary education policy, 37
culpability, 36
cultural exclusion, 20
cultural resources, 79, 92
culture, 14, 15, 17, 22, 29, 34, 37, 48, 72, 80, 98, 105
    of poverty, 22
    and power, 34
curriculum
    assessment, 67, 104
    frameworks, 41
    relevance, 67

D

damaged, 2, 7, 34, 40, 56, 63, 66, 91
damaging
    effects of schooling, 3
    impact, 36, 42
deficiencies, 1, 14, 60
deficit and pathologizing portrayals, 38
deficit thinking, 21, 23, 35, 36, 42
deficits, 17, 20–23, 35, 36, 38, 42, 47, 50, 90, 98, 106, 112
degradation, 109
delinquency, 110
deliverable performance targets, 11, 110
demanding work, 82
democracy, 11
democratic scrutiny, 105
democratization of education, 107, 108
denial, 106
depreciation, 106
detached, 32, 110
devaluation, 106

Subject Index

dialectical theory building, 31
dialogic
    approach, 84
    portraits, 38
    relationship, 33
dialogue and negotiation, 72
didactic or transmission model of teaching, 84
disadvantage 1, 2, 17, 19, 23, 29, 32, 35, 36, 43, 47, 74, 103, 109, 112
disaffected young people, 8, 47, 49, 81
disaffection, 4, 8, 34, 37, 45, 47, 49, 81
disciplinary requirements, 18
disconnected, 20, 21, 42, 47, 48, 102, 105, 108, 110, 112
disconnecting from schooling, 1, 3, 4, 20, 41
discriminatory policies, 33, 40, 90
diseased reasoning, 22
disenfranchisement, 107
disengage, 17, 20–22, 30, 32, 37, 43, 45, 67, 72, 82, 94, 95, 102, 105–107
disillusionment, 107
dispirited adolescents, 42
displacement, 7, 21, 102
dispossession, 17
doing
    policy, 10
    theory critically, 111
domestic violence, 30, 42, 92, 95
dominant groups, 19
dress code, 18, 67, 107
drug addiction, 30

E

economic
    forms of capital, 103
    fundamentalism, 10
    independence, 49, 52
    interest, 10, 13
    rationalism, 10
educability, 23
educational
    aptitude, 104
    credentials, 103
    equality, 99
    impediment, 106
    policy, 10, 24, 32, 99, 111
    privileging, 105
    re-engagement, 5, 102
    relationships, 109
    resources, 104
elite occupations, 23
embedded interviews, 31
emotional
    capabilities, 109
    effective, 107
    scars of schooling, 77
    social and cultural identities, 99
    social lives, 89
emotions, 59, 109, 110
employment, 9, 12, 29, 43, 45, 46, 49, 52, 63, 66, 74, 76, 81, 84, 94, 98
engaging
    disaffected students, 47, 67, 81
    pedagogies, 49, 66, 67, 70
equality
    of condition, 102, 103, 106, 107, 110
    of power, 107
erosion of civility, 25
estrangement, 37
ethical issues, 33
ethnicity, 19, 81
ethnographic
    interviews, 4, 29, 31, 33
    research, 28, 31, 32
eugenics, 104
Every Child Matters, 7
evidence-based knowledge, 15
exclusion, 4, 13, 15, 16, 19, 20, 21, 37, 56, 63, 71, 92, 107, 108, 111, 112
extended participant responses, 32

F

factory model of schooling, 83
failure, 8, 13, 31, 37, 38, 50, 71, 79, 81, 97, 98, 103, 105, 106, 108
false dichotomies, 106
family
    life, 91

relationships, 56, 94
fear, 13, 20, 56, 67, 109
finding the hooks, 84, 85
fixing individual students, 21
flexible
    approach to learning, 30, 43, 68
    learning centers, 42, 49, 80, 97
freedom, 18, 28, 49, 52, 55, 70, 72
frustration, 37
fugitive notions, 106
fun, 60, 70, 71

G

gender, 37, 106
geographies of exclusion, 16, 19
getting a job, 52
ghettoization, 19
ghettos of advantage, 103
giving up on school, 101
global forces, 111
go the extra yards, 76
good
    ethnography, 38
    teachers, 84, 109, 110

H

hands-on learning, 23, 45, 55, 58, 67, 70, 71, 85, 87
hanging in, 86
hapless victims, 11, 79
harassment, 18, 37, 42, 56, 60, 63, 64
having
    a reputation, 59
    a say, 72
health, 3, 31, 33, 37, 39, 44, 45, 47, 53, 62, 65, 66, 68, 74, 80, 86, 91, 93–99
hegemonic curriculum, 43, 47
hegemony, 36, 44
hidden market forces, 11
hierarchical decision-making, 84
high school, 29, 30, 44, 46, 47, 49, 56, 58–60, 64, 69, 70, 71, 73, 79, 80, 83, 85, 87, 104, 115
high stakes testing, 12, 74
holistic approach, 94, 99

homelessness, 30, 42, 92, 93, 95
honoring voices, 37
hope, 2, 3, 31, 32, 34, 36–38, 40, 42, 52, 58, 60, 77, 81, 82, 83, 93, 109, 112
Hopi Indians, 9
house of fear, 13
human
    capital, 48
    spirit, 50
humanizing relationships, 49, 56, 57 81, 89

I

identity, 2, 12, 37, 38, 43, 46, 48, 49, 52, 54, 56, 66, 79, 87, 91, 110
ideology, 10, 11, 21, 23
imaginative space, 10
IMF, 15
impediments, 62, 80, 81, 106
improving education and life chances, 89
incentives, 24, 94
inclusion, 19, 107
indifference, 9, 111
indigenous forms of knowledge, 15
individual learning plans, 44, 45, 82, 86–89
individualism, 12, 17
individualizing
    problems, 103
    responsibility, 12, 106
inequality, 4, 5, 21, 24, 34, 79, 91, 97, 101, 102, 104, 105, 107, 110
inequitable distribution of benefits, 34
informants' lives, 36
injustices, 90
insider
    knowledge, 31, 42
    stories, 37
institution of schooling, 2, 21
institutional
    intolerance, 111
    memory, 15
    power, 54
    practices of schools, 98
institutionalized inequality, 22, 105
instrumental, 17, 47, 84

Subject Index

integrated and collective approaches, 92
intelligence, 47, 104, 105
interactive trouble, 108
interferences and obstacles, 112
inter-generational, 20, 23
interpretive tradition, 36
interrupting the status quo, 14
intimidation, 37, 60
islands of decency, 90

J

joys of teaching, 86
juvenile justice, 92, 94

K

labor market, 17, 37, 49
lack of connection, 30, 47, 87
language and space to talk, 110
leadership training, 25
league tables, 110
learning as multi-dimensional, 99
learning centers, 27, 41, 44, 45, 59, 62, 66, 67, 73, 74, 76, 79, 80, 97
life chances, 3, 32–34, 63, 89
life history of students, 87
life-saving, 54, 56, 74, 90, 91
local solutions, 112
loss of public space, 16
love, 41, 102, 109
low socioeconomic backgrounds, 30, 81
low-skill, low-paid, insecure, work, 12, 49

M

mainstream schools, 3, 30, 42, 43, 46, 47, 49, 54, 59, 66, 74, 80, 84, 87
managerialism, 2
manual or semi-skilled jobs, 20, 23
marginalized, 2, 3, 7, 28, 42, 82, 92, 95, 97, 98, 104, 107, 108
markets, 11, 17, 18, 25, 37, 49, 103, 104
material deprivation, 16
meaningful learning, 42
measurement, 18, 106, 107

of intelligence, 104
mental retardation, 22
middle class, 11, 13, 76, 81, 92, 103, 105
middle school pedagogy, 43
militarized culture, 4, 110
mindless intrusion, 13
misrecognition, 106
misrepresentation, 107
moral
    dimension, 40
    panic, 8, 19
    responsibility, 34
multi-skilled workforce, 10
multivocal conversations, 38
muscular
    policies, 2, 7, 20, 110, 112
    targets, 110
mutual respect, 56, 57
myth-busting, 66

N

narrative research, 28
narratives of exclusion, 19
negotiation, 35, 61, 72, 73
neighborhood
    house, 27, 30, 45, 58
    safety, 91
    schools, 25
neighborhoods, 1, 16, 19, 20, 25, 27, 29, 30, 44, 45, 58, 61, 64, 91
neoliberalism, 11, 12, 17, 23, 24, 42, 63, 112, 113
New Right, 10
No Child Left Behind, 7
norms of students' behavior, 87

O

obedience training school, 90
obstacles in returning to learning, 32
OECD, 15
one-on-one talk, 57
opportunities for social learning, 89
oppositional ideas, 14, 37
oppression, 14, 21, 22, 34, 40, 42, 111
opting out of school, 110

overcoming anger, 81
ownership, 54, 72, 107

P

paradoxes and contradictions, 18
parental neglect, 95
parenting skills, 20, 81
parents, 5, 8, 11, 13, 17, 23, 30, 32, 43, 44, 62–66, 71–75, 84, 88–92, 96, 97, 103–105
participants' perspectives, 31
participative opportunities, 18
participatory social vision, 48
passion for learning, 4, 42
paternalistic responses, 36
pedagogic relationships, 82
pedagogy
    assessment, 107
    disconnection, 112
    reconnection, 112
performativity measures, 2
personal
    capital, 91
    portfolio, 46
personalized learning, 30
pits of despair, 3
place-based learning, 37
points of engagement, 84
policy
    blindness and deafness, 2
    fixes, 41
    frameworks, 98
    and practice, 101
    regimes, 28, 34, 40, 103
    transfers, 15
political
    imagination, 18
    laden terms, 35
    research, 34
    structures, 99
politics of non-engagement, 7
poor and culturally diverse children, 81
popular culture, 37
portraits, 29, 35, 37–40, 42, 52, 53, 59, 61, 65, 70–73, 75, 76, 77, 80, 83, 86, 89, 90, 93–97
portraiture, 4, 31, 37, 38, 39, 42, 111
positive
    reinforcement, 86
    sense of identity, 46
positive elements of engagement, 37
positivist, 5, 34, 110
poverty, 11, 16, 22, 25, 37, 42, 91, 98, 101, 108, 112
power, 4, 8, 18, 19, 22, 25, 28, 32, 34, 36, 37, 38, 54, 55, 72, 73, 102, 107, 108, 111
predatory consumption industry, 110
pregnant or parenting teenagers, 37, 63
privatization, 16, 17
privileged in society, 105
pro-active work, 95
problem students, 98
professional judgment, 108
profit-seeking enterprises, 25
programmatic solutions, 8, 11
pseudoscience, 22
public
    ethnography, 35
    policy, 16, 20, 63
    spaces, 19, 112
punctuality, 107
punitive, 56, 72, 90
purposeful
    conversations, 31, 32
    lives, 31
pushed out of school, 3, 30

Q

quality, 10, 18, 23, 107

R

race, 19, 83
racism, 34, 37, 42, 61, 62, 101
radical reformers, 14
recalcitrant young people, 20
recognition, 81, 102, 106, 107
reconnection and re-engagement, 2, 5, 31, 33, 43–46, 48, 57, 61, 66, 70, 73, 74, 76, 77, 80, 81, 86, 87, 89, 91, 101, 111, 115
re-engagement programs, 31, 43–46, 57, 73, 74, 76, 77, 81, 86, 87, 91, 115

Subject Index

re-entry program, 27, 29–33, 37, 50, 54, 56, 57, 60, 61
reform imposed on schools, 8, 9, 13, 91
re-inventing young lives, 77, 107
relational
    burden, 110
    conversations, 8
    learning, 57, 81, 110
    lives, 108
    nature of teachers' work, 109
    school, 109
    trust, 57, 86, 97
relationships, 18, 30, 32, 37, 43, 47, 49, 56, 57, 59, 62, 69, 82, 94, 95, 98, 107–111
relevance of schooling and curriculum, 2, 3, 31, 40, 46, 47, 51, 67
research
    craft, 4, 28
    as praxis, 40, 38
    reciprocity, 35
researcher's perspective, 39
researching for/with, 35
resilience, 36, 77
resistance, 37
resources, 45, 46, 48, 49, 62, 63, 66, 73, 79, 87, 92, 97, 101, 103–107, 110
respect, 32, 37, 49, 52, 55–58, 62, 63, 68, 102, 106–108
re-thinking educational policy, 99
re-writing conditions of learning, 111
risk taking, 106
Rousseauian glass, 14
rules, sanctions and regulations, 24, 49, 54, 56, 67, 83, 84, 107, 111
ruthless economy, 10, 119

S

school
    choice, 11, 12, 103
    as coercive institution, 56
    connectedness, 43, 47
    drop-outs, 21, 30, 37, 72, 92
    effectiveness, 15
    engagement from student perspective, 98
    reform, 9, 13, 91
    retention, 43, 92, 98
    as uncaring place, 47
scientific evidence-based research, 28
second-chance education, 98
segregation and disability, 107
selection and admission, 103
self
    discipline, 20, 50
    education, 90
    seeking enterprises, 12
semi-skilled work, 20, 23
semi-structured interviews, 32
sense of connection, 62, 82
sexism, 34, 37
sexual abuse, 95
sexual harassment, 42
sexuality, 96, 106
shared responsibility, 57
shrill rhetoric, 17, 21
significant others, 5, 31, 33, 77, 80, 84, 91, 99, 110
silence, 3, 11, 28, 73, 106
silent witnesses, 79
skills for social living, 30
smaller classes, 59, 69
snake-oil salesmen, 10
social
    capital, 76
    class, 20, 37, 81, 103–106
    connectedness, 5
    Darwinism, 11, 21
    imaginary, 112
    isolation, 63
    learning, 16, 74, 89
    networks, 49, 63, 64, 91, 103
    public policy, 16
    skills, 46, 95
    space, 16
    stratification, 21
socially
    constructed, 21, 49
    critical, 33
    damaged, 66
    just, 5, 113
societal inequalities, 16

soft revolution, 113
solidarity, 102, 109
sorting and sifting, 107
space, 3, 10, 16, 18, 19, 20, 23, 28, 39, 40, 66, 68, 70, 81, 90, 97, 103, 112
spaces for participation, 18
speaking
    back, 35, 79, 90, 112
    out, 34
    the unpleasant, 111
special needs, 45, 46, 62
spirit of hope, 83
stand-alone profit centers, 110
standards, 2, 9, 41, 67
starting afresh, 59, 83
stereotypes, 22, 36, 38, 42, 63, 106
stigma, 63, 64, 66, 79
stories of young people, 24
storylines, 4, 32, 39, 40, 41, 111
streaming practices, 56, 104
structural inequalities, 76
structure and management, 25
structured
    interviews, 32
    learning opportunities, 32
student
    control over learning, 32, 41, 48, 50, 53, 54–56, 107
    detachment, 110
students living independently, 62
    histories and experiences, 87
    who have opted out, 87
substance abuse, 107, 110
success
    and failure, 37
    stories, 76, 89, 95
support networks, 62, 89, 96
suspension, 37
switched-off learners, 42
systematic bias, 106

T

talents, 52, 98
targeted populations, 35
teacher effectiveness, 15, 86
teacher-proof packages, 84
teachers' stories, 80
    work, 46, 84, 109. 110
teacher-student interaction, 13, 84, 108
teaching as a complex activity, 86
teamwork, 95
technical schools, 104
technologies of exclusion, 56
tectonic plates of capitalism, 8
teenage mothers, 42, 63, 64, 66
tensions and contradictions, 4, 5, 28
testing, 2, 12, 17, 25, 56, 74, 84, 97, 104, 105
toxic effects of inequality, 79
tracking, 85, 104
traditional schools, 30, 35, 67, 97
transformative, 42, 47, 48, 98
    intellectuals, 98
transiting to employment, 12
transparency, 105, 106
triangulation or validation, 5
trivialization, 107
troublemakers, 30, 95
troubling questions, 4, 23
true believer, 25
trust, 5, 10, 25, 49, 56, 57, 59, 61, 62, 69–71, 82, 86, 89, 90, 96, 97, 106, 108

U

unauthorized methods, 81, 83
uncaring places, 56
uncertain enterprise, 86
uneasy closure, 111
uneducable, 22
unemployment, 29
unequal schooling outcomes, 34
unfair system, 101
unjust structures and policies, 22, 34, 36, 87, 89, 109
unpleasant realities, 3, 4, 8
unsettling dominant beliefs, 20
unwarranted conclusions, 22
uplifting and positive accounts, 3
user-pays, 10

V

valued social ends, 10
value-free research, 34
vandalized, 9, 53
vernacular forms of expression, 105
vested interest group, 106
victim, 11, 19, 20, 21, 30, 35–37, 56, 79, 112
    blaming, 20, 21, 121
    construction, 19, 120
victimization, 37
Vietnam War, 13
vignette, 40
violence, 30, 42, 60, 95
visions of success, 81
vocational aspirations, 54
    tracking, 104
vocationalism, 12, 20, 23, 37, 54, 64, 76, 104
voice, 1, 3, 15, 16, 21, 25, 27, 28, 29, 31, 32, 37, 39, 40, 42, 48, 49, 71, 73, 77, 79, 89
voiced research, 28, 31
Voices from the Margins, 25

W

welfare
    dependency, 29
    support, 97
well-being, 45, 62, 66, 74, 82
Wingspread Conference, 47
witnesses, 111
working
    class, 12, 23, 103, 104
    part-time, 108
World Bank, 15
world's best practice, 10
wounded by school, 31, 42, 50, 77

Y

young parenthood, 39, 44, 62–66, 74, 75, 86, 90, 96
young people's
    exclusion, 16
    identities, 15, 33, 37, 99
    narratives, 36, 47, 72, 79
youth housing, 31, 92, 93
youth unemployment, 49, 76

Z

zero tolerance, 19, 56

Author Index

A

Anderson, G., 35
Angus, L., 34, 109
Anyon, J., 36
Apple, M., 34
Ayers, W., iv, 89, 90

B

Bailey, C., 35
Baker, J., 102–110
Bernstein, B., 105
Bessant, J., 31
Beutel, D., 82
Blum, R., 47
Bourdieu, P., 106
Brown, P., 23
Bryk, A., 57
Burgess, R., 32

C

Camus, A., 17
Carspecken, P., 34
Cervini, E., 104
Chamberlain, C., 92
Chapman, T., 38
Chavez, R., 7, 111
Connell, B., 109
Costello, T., 9

D

Darling-Hammond, L., 83
Davis, J., 66
Delpit, L., 81
Denzin, N., 28
Dewey, J., 56
Dixon, A., 38
Down, B., 22, 34, 79, 87, 109
Duffy, K., 16
Dunkley, C., 16, 19, 20

E

Ennew, J., 19

F

Fine, M., 35
Fitzgerald, T., 34

Foley, D., 35
Foucault, M., 56
Freebody, P., 108

G

Giroux, H., 49, 56, 98
Goodman, J., 36
Green, N., 38
Griffiths, M., 35
Gunn, S., 108

H

Hattam, R., 92, 109
Head, S., 10
Hickling-Hudson, H., 15
Hinson, G., 35
Hutchby, I., 35

J

Jones, R., 104

K

Keynes, J., 24
Kincheloe, J., 83, 86
Kozol, J., 13, 35

L

Lather, P., 35, 40
Lawrence-Lightfoot, S., 38, 77
Lodge, A., 108
Lubeck, S., 36
Lucas, B., 87
Ludwig, C., 108
Lynch, K., 102–110

M

MacKenzie, D., 92
Madison, D., 34, 35
McGregor, C., 67
McInerney, P., 22, 34, 35, 39, 79, 87, 109
Millei, T., 61
Mills, C.W., 17

Mills, M., 67
Moore, B., 35
Moran-Ellis, J., 35
Morrow, V., 18, 19

N

Nagge, J., 21
Nagle, J., 25
Noguera, P., 57

O

O'Donnell, J., 7, 111
Olson, K., 31, 50, 77
Osterman, K., 56

P

Palmer, P., 87
Passeron, J., 106
Payne, R., 22
Phillips, R., 91
Pittaway, S., 63
Polesel, J., 76
Postman, N., 13–15
Prosser, B., 87

R

Ravitch, D., 24, 25
Reid, A., 87, 109
Rose, M., 86
Rowe, P., 92, 99
Ryan, W., 21

S

Savelsberg, H., 92, 99
Schneider, A., 57
Sen, A., 49
Shacklock, J., 9, 10, 109
Shor, I., 54
Sibley, D., 16, 19, 20
Sloan, T., 111
Smyth, J., 9, 10, 22, 31, 34, 35, 39, 49, 72, 79, 87, 92, 109, 110